KILLING *of*
AFRICAN-
AMERICANS
BY RACIST COPS

JOHN OSOM, MSP

authorHOUSE®

AuthorHouse™
1663 Liberty Drive
Bloomington, IN 47403
www.authorhouse.com
Phone: 1 (800) 839-8640

Published by AuthorHouse   10/05/2016

ISBN: 978-1-5246-2476-7 (sc)
ISBN: 978-1-5246-2474-3 (hc)
ISBN: 978-1-5246-2475-0 (e)

Library of Congress Control Number: 2016913333

Print information available on the last page.

This book is printed on acid-free paper.

KJV
Scripture quotations marked KJV are from the Holy Bible, King James Version
(Authorized Version). First published in 1611. Quoted from the KJV Classic
Reference Bible, Copyright © 1983 by The Zondervan Corporation.

ESV
Unless otherwise indicated, all scripture quotations are from The Holy Bible,
English Standard Version® (ESV®). Copyright ©2001 by Crossway Bibles, a
division of Good News Publishers. Used by permission. All rights reserved.

NIV
Scripture quotations marked NIV are taken from the Holy Bible, New
International Version®. NIV®. Copyright © 1973, 1978, 1984 by International
Bible Society. Used by permission of Zondervan. All rights reserved.

Dedication

To fellow Americans especially African-Americans killed by Police Officers on the streets of this nation due to racial hatred. May the merciful God have mercy on you and rest your dear souls in peace. Amen.

Foreword

Having spent over thirty years of my life in God's own country called United States of America (USA), I find it gratifying that an immigrant resident like myself can summon the courage to put on record some of the misconceptions and a microcosm of the blatant human rights abuses suffered by African-Americans and other people of "color" in the hands of police. It is about time the truth be told, the world be educated, and misrepresentation of facts be revealed.

The courage by Rev Fr. (Dr) John Osom to bring this to fore, from a pedagogical perspective is welcome. I admire his tutorial in explaining the misuse of terms and the colorization and demonetization of fellow humans with "red blood" so as to justify immoral and satanic practice of slavery, which over hundred years was of physical torment, of which today has become mental torture. Rev. Fr. Osom has taken pains to research for facts and calibrated his observations from human dignity point of view. His comments, tutorials, and anecdotal observations can be controversial to the "master schemers" and enemies of human dignity. Most cited in this dehumanizing practice are the police. I am not surprised. My wife has been a victim of a simple traffic offense, who under pregnancy, she was taken to a jail cell without given any opportunity to call me (the husband) or access to a public defender. She was verbally abused. Just may be, the pregnancy was respected,who knows what could have happen to her. They were all white policemen. This is just one incident. I can as well follow Rev. Fr. Osom to talk about human right abuses by police in USA.

The tittle of the book: 'African-Americans Killed by racist Cops' is appropriate but the contents do not contain the full story. As a priest, I believe Rev Fr. Osom tries to be modest, less con-frontal, and politely assertive. I like his major premise of the book. As a teacher and a man of God, he seeks "to correct the erroneous classification of people into black and white by pointing out that though various races are endowed with different complexions no human beings are neither white nor black." African-Americans have various degrees of brown complexion or color while the Caucasians have pale and not white complexion. The book highlights that no particular color or complexion is superior to the other. Besides this, to refer to African-Americans as people of color does not make sense since, in the first place, no human being is colorless unless one is referring to those in the spirit world. Thus for the racist Caucasian police officers to use color as a basis to be committing murder under the guise of protecting their lives is a betrayal of their profession of protecting lives and property on the road. The book makes proposals towards addressing the issue raised.

The contents of this book can be used in human relation training for police and civil peace keeping agencies in countries which unintentionally or knowingly practice the dehumanizing acts enumerated by Rev. Fr. Osom. The book is simple to read and facts cited are ubiquitous in print and digital media, in words, photographs, and video in many cases. The book is not indicting the police agencies to appear in court. Simply, stop brutalizing and dehumanizing people of black race, or any race for that matter, in USA. Lets all be civil and "get along" as one body with multicultural views.

Acknowledgement

As the saying goes, 'no single tree makes a forest'. Consequently this work has some people working behind the scene, helping to bring it to its publication level. So I am most grateful to Deacon Larry Oney in the Archdiocese of New Orleans and his friend who gladly accepted not only to proof-read the text but also made useful suggestions regarding the adjustment of the chapters of this book. I am equally grateful to Father Ifiok Udofia, Msp, the editor of our Ambassador Magazine in Nigeria, for taking part of his vacation visit to the United States to correct some typographical errors in the book. Finally I thank Father Raphael Obotama for his useful advice in the choice of Author House for the publication of this book.

Contents

Chapter One

Chapter Two

Chapter Three

Chapter Four

Chapter Five

Introduction

Experience reveals that nobody was, is or will ever be happy when he or she is being discriminated against irrespective of any race the individual comes from or happens to be categorized into. Obviously the root cause of compartmentalizing human beings is selfishness coupled with inability to accept one's limitations. This inevitably leads some people to the unfounded belief that their particular complexion is superior and to treat others as inferior. Even if such a thing could have been tolerated in the past, the emergence of new scientific discoveries, makes this make- belief superior complex ridiculous. This write-up aims to examine the current manifestations of racism, which often results in the killing or incarceration of many young African- Americans by some Caucasian police officers while under the pretext of doing their duty of safe-guarding the public on the road.

Chapter one examines the historical perspective regarding the original inhabitants of America as well as the subsequent arrival of immigrants from different parts of the world, beginning with the Britons. After receiving the hospitality of Native Americans, some Britons not only turn against the natives, but also brought in African-Americans as slaves to work for them on their plantations particularly in the Southern part of the country. This continued until the civil war put an end to the obnoxious trade and exploitations of fellow human beings as slaves.

Chapter two delves into the various pigmentations characteristic of different races, consisting initially of three sections: the Caucasians or pale skinned people originating mostly from Europe; the Mongolians or yellow skinned people from Asia; the dark or brown skinned people found in most parts of Africa. A more detailed categorization of human beings based on their races was later compiled by Johann Friedrich Blumenbach, a German anthropologist. He expanded homo sapiens into five distinct races based on their physical characteristics: the Mongolians or yellow skinned people; the red race (under which he included the Native Americans); the Brown Malayan race; the Black Ethiopian race and the Caucasians, based on the shape of their skulls. This shape is assumed by some to be the determinant characteristic or phrenology. However, not only had Blumenbach never introduce any hierarchy but he vehemently protested against any stress on racial hierarchies raised by his colleagues both in his university and elsewhere in Europe. Since there was no rational justification for the introduction of hierarchy and superiority/ inferiority complexes between the so called 'while and black' races, it is compared to the invention of the first television set in which every picture was seen either as white or black on the screen.

This misconception regarding the superiority of the Caucasian complexion erroneously termed "white" and-- the dark or brown complexion erroneously-- termed "black" is singled out as the reason why some Caucasian police officers embark on the elimination of some African-Americans road users in this county –it hearkens back to the slave trade era. Some practical examples of African-Americans shot and killed on the road with no rational justifications are cited in this chapter to affirm the fact that many of these African-Americans are killed for reasons other than traffic violations.

Chapter Three affirms that, to some extent, there are noticeable elements of some African American teachers putting down students of their same race under the guise of discipline. It also delves into the fact that, though a few from a particular race might be technologically gifted, it does not in any way indicate that they are of a superior race. The superiority complex is responsible for many other abnormalities committed, such as abnormal sexual relationships between members of the same gender. Finally this chapter discusses the case of Rachel Dolezan, a Caucasian woman who claims to be African American. While everyone is supposed to be at home with one's own race, treating others with respect, it does not make sense if, in an attempt to interact with people from another race one pretends to be a member of that race.

Chapter Four cites some examples of Caucasian police officers who had killed innocent African-Americans being brought to court and found guilty but being bailed out with the tax payers' money. It highlights the fact that a double injustice is done to the nation: the families of the diseased are deprived of their loved ones, and public income is used to bail out a culprit, even though the individual was employed by the state. Besides this, by unnecessarily harassing the innocent people based on their complexion, the culprit Caucasian police officers are not only ineffective in the job which they are paid by the state to do, but also deprive themselves and the entire police force of the public trust they need to be able to carry out their duties effectively. No one in the community assigned to them would be eager to entrust them with legitimate information anymore.

The chapter cites example of African American police officers who, when not on duty for easy identification, are equally harassed or even beaten up by their Caucasian colleagues on duty while on the road. Some Caucasian attorneys are even co-conspirators with these Caucasian police officers in the elimination of the African American victims.

Apart from the road harassment, racism abounds in other sectors such as employment opportunities for qualified African-Americans, housing etc.

Chapter Five suggests some proposals aimed at minimizing racial discriminations. It highlights the fact that only a minimal percentage of the Caucasian police officers are guilty of this racial discrimination or racial profiling on the roads while the majority of them are fair-minded and as such discharge their duties effectively. An extensive psychological analysis was undertaken which showed that everyone, by reason of being human, has some form of hidden racism or tribalism. However, once it is discovered and the individual made aware of it via training, it can be minimized. A necessary link between racism and biases is also highlighted in this chapter.

Chapter One

Discrimination of one race against another should have by now been confined to history books, to the ignorance of the past.

There is no denying that, during the pre-scientific era when it was either not possible or difficult for one race to interact or even communicate with another, there were mutual suspicions and fairy-tales told about different races. Some of these stories were scaring and so formed basis for distrust. Allow me to cite a couple of examples here. First, I can still recall one of my classmates in 1982 telling me that while he was in grade school, one of his class-mates was brought to the principal for fighting in the rest room with his Caucasian class-mate. The child had wanted to see his tail, since he was told by his parents that people of African descent had tails like monkeys.

Second, I remember something that happened to me in 1985 during my post graduate studies in Rome. When I was going to help out in a parish at Easter celebration, some of the children who had obviously never seen any person of my brown complexion, came over following the celebration. They talked with me, and held and examined my hands to see if there would be any mark from my hands left in theirs. These two stories from different settings indicate the willingness of children, in their innocence, to step out from their enclosure to look for facts, not just the fairy tales they are saddled with. The question here is this: if children can embark on this fact- finding strategy, why should adults prefer to remain comfortable in their ignorance rather than recognizing the fact that, just as there are varieties of things to make life much more meaningful, so are there people from different races created by God, differing in size, charisma, colors or complexions, or any other endowments. Besides this, in this contemporary global village of ours, where all means of knowledge is made available for those who care to know, it has become obvious that the worth of any human being does not depend on which part of the globe the individual was born or on his/her complexion but the type of human being, good or bad he/she chooses to be.

AMERICAN Background Check: There is no justification for anyone to be a Racist

In this country, we know that before someone is hired for any reasonable job background check is of utmost importance. In this context, we are going to examine the background check not of individuals but of the country itself to show that there is no justification for someone to be a racist. Historically it is a well-known fact that the original inhabitants, the owners of this land are the Indian Americans (Native Americans) who, initially happily welcomed immigrants from Europe and helped them to settle and cultivate the land. Unfortunately they were gradually sidelined by the very guests who, through technology had access to weapons with which the Native Americans were pushed aside and consequently confined to a small section of the country. They were considered too primitive to be allowed to mingle with the "enlightened or civilized Europeans". The Obama's administration is now realistically incorporating their culture into the mainstream of this country. For example in 2013, Obama appointed a Native American woman to serve as federal judge.

There is no doubt that the fertility of the land brought about the negative and long standing injustice of the American enslavement of the unfortunate Africans brought in chains into this country. Beginning in the 16th century, Africans were brought to cultivate the land for the Caucasians, since they were naturally endowed with strength with which to till the ground and conquer it (Gen.1: 28). Before delving into how African-Americans were actually brought and forced into the country as slaves, it is important to briefly examine how the immigrants from Europe first kept Native Americans as slaves.

Conflicts of the European immigrants with the Native - Americans

From the end of the 15th century, the emigration of those of European extraction to the Americas led to centuries of conflicts and adjustment periods between the immigrants and the natives. Many Native Americans lived as hunter gatherer societies and preserved their history in oral tradition and artwork. Therefore the first written accounts of conflict were authored by European immigrants. As would be expected, the indigenous cultures were quite different from those of proto-industrial immigrants. These differences, along with the shifting alliances among different nations at the time caused extensive political tension, ethnic violence and social disruption.

Following the revolt of the then colonies against Britain, President George Washington and Henry Knox conceived the idea of "civilizing" Native Americans in preparation for assimilation as US citizens either voluntarily-- as with Choctaw-- or by force. The expansion of the European American populations to the west following the American revolution resulted in increased pressure on Native American lands, warfare between groups and rising tensions. In 1830 the US congress passed the Indian Removal Act authorizing the government to relocate Native Americans from their own lands within the established states to lands west of the Mississippi River to accommodate the European American expansion. This led to the near genocide of many tribes, with brutally forced marches known as the trial of tears. It was the establishment of the treaty rights that eventually allowed the Indian Americans to gradually embrace formal education through which they developed cultural activism in the late 1960's and political participation. This led to expanding efforts to teach and preserve indigenous languages for younger generations as well as infrastructures. More recently Native Americans have founded

4

independent newspapers and online media including, the first Native American television channel, Native American studies programs, tribal schools- including universities and museums, and language programs. Several Native Americans have also become published authors.

Slavery in the Americas

Prior to the advent of European immigrants into the U.S., the Native Americans often had tribal wars among themselves, and captured men from the warfronts as slaves. The slaves were eventually integrated into the tribes in which they were brought. At times such captive slaves were made to fill in the gaps left by the men killed during the war. Initially when the Europeans arrived America, some of these slaves were sold to them by tribal warriors to work on the Europeans' farms. Slavery in America first began in April 1502 when the Spanish colonist transported the first Africans forced into slavery and brought in chains to Hispaniola. [1] This mark the initial contact of the Native Americans with Africans. The bone of contention between the African-Americans and the Native Americans surfaced when the former coming in initially as traders gained favor with the Europeans. Following the ensuing envy in which the Cherokee exhibited the strongest color prejudice of all Native Americans, it was contended that because of the European fears of a possible united revolt of the Native Americans and African slaves, the colonist encouraged hostility between the two groups: "Whites sought to convince the Native Americans that African-Americans worked against their best interest". [2]

In 1751 South Carolina Law stated :"The carrying of the negroes among the Indians has all along been thought detrimental, as an intimacy ought to be avoided ". In addition, in 1758 the governor of South Carolina, James Glen, wrote:

> "It has always been the policy of this government to create an aversion in them, Indians to Negroes. The two groups considered inferior by the Europeans were made to work and live together (as slaves to the Europeans), produced collective recipes for food, shared herbal remedies, myths and legends and in the end intermarried. Due to the shortage of men, many tribes encouraged marriage between the two groups to create stronger, healthier children from the unions"[3].

Since the 18th century, many Native American women married the run-away African men due to the decreased in the population of men in Native American villages.[4] Some of the Native American women, due to the matrilineal family system, bought male African slaves but, unknown to the Europeans, freed and married these African men into their tribes. According to the principle of partus sequitur ventrem, which the colonists incorporated in to the law, when the African men married and had children with their Native American wives, the children so born were freed since the mother was free.

The Initial attempt at abolishing Negroes slavery

It was only after more than three centuries (from 1504 to 1863) of enslaving the people from Africa that it gradually dawned on some politicians that such obnoxious trade should be stopped. This is attributed to be one of the causes of the civil war fought between the Northern and Southern parts of the country. In January 1963, President Abraham Lincoln issued an Emancipation Proclamation setting free all the slaves engaged in the civil war. Though it was only limited to the slaves conscripted to fight on the side of the Union, the proclamation marked an important point of departure in American history. It is believed that at least in theory, slavery came to an end with the passage of the Thirteen Amendment to the Constitution on December 1865 passed by Congress on January 31st and ratified by the states on December 6th. It abolished slavery in the United States and provided that "Neither slavery nor involuntary servitude except as punishment for crime whereof the party shall have been duly convicted, shall exist within the United State or any place subject to her jurisdiction. This amendment was passed at the end of the civil war before the Southern States were restored to the Union. Though it had been passed by the Senate on April 1864, it was only through the intervention of President Lincoln that it was added to the Republican Platform for the upcoming presidential election. That consequently convinced the House (Congress) to finally pass the bill on January31st,1865 with a vote of 119-56. The following day, February 1st, Lincoln approved the joined resolution of Congress and submitted the proposed amendment to the states' legislatures whose necessary majority number ratified it on December 6th, 1865.

The slaves trade mentality continue to manifest itself from 1865 till now, with the rise of racial discrimination in nearly all sectors of American life. Before delving into the intricacies of discrimination in various categories, it is important to peruse key phases in the struggles that African-Americans, those affected the most in the fight for freedom, have been enduring for all people now living in this county.

1964 Civil Right Act

Prior to his assassination in 1963, President John F. Kennedy, proposed a Civil Right Bill aimed at putting an end to the segregation of African-Americans from Caucasians in public facilities and transportation such as schools, restaurants, train, busses, Churches, and a host of others. In 1964, President Lyndon B. Johnson convinced the Americans that the time had come to address the segregation problem. With the increasing number of African-Americans in cities the Caucasians started passing restrictive laws demarcating urban spaces within racial lines. As if this was not enough, they also instituted the "separate but equal law". When a mixed race thirty year old shoemaker, Homer Plessy violated the Louisiana separate Car Act delineating separate train cars for "white and Black" passengers in 1892, the case was taken to the Supreme Court. The court upheld the law favored by a 7 – 1 vote "as long as the facilities were separate but equal". This became known as the Jim Crow law. However it is worth noting that the only dissenting vote was cast by Justice John Marshall Harlan. In defense of Plessy, he protested that his colleagues were wrongly favoring the existing segregation. He said:

> "Our constitution is color blind and neither knows nor tolerates classes among citizens. The arbitrary separation of citizens on the bases of race while they are on public highway is a badge of servitude wholly inconsistent with the civil freedom and equality before the law established by the Constitution. It can never be justified upon any legal ground".[5]

This had to be challenged in court since the facilities were never equal in 1954. Gradually it led to the Montgomery bus boycott in 1955 and sit-inns of 1960 as well as the Freedom Rides of 1961. As more and more African-Americans risked their lives exposing the harshness of the racial laws in the wake of the Brown decision, the federal Government along with the president could no longer ignore segregation. It is against this backdrop that President Johnson, as indicated above, announced his intention to push a Civil Right Bill: "...no memorial oration or eulogy could more eloquently honor President Kennedy's memory than the earliest possible passage of the civil rights bill for which he fought so long. We have talked for a hundred years or more. It is time now to write the next chapter and to write it in the books of law".[6]

President Johnson received the needed votes in congress enabling him to sign the bill into law in July,1964. The first part of the legislation states that its purpose is "to enforce the constitutional right to vote, to confer jurisdiction upon the district courts of the United States to provide injunctive relief against discrimination in public accommodation, to authorize the Attorney General to institute suits, to protect facilities and public education, to extend the commission on civil Rights, to prevent discrimination in federal assisted programs, to establish a commission on Equal Employment Opportunity and other purposes"[7].

The main purpose of the Act was to end the piecemeal strategy of integration by putting an end once and for all to Jim Crow law which has created legalized discrimination that lasted for over 60 years.

The Effects of the 1964 Civil Rights Acts

While in the South, the Caucasians were still maneuvering the legal and extra legal means to deprive African-Americans living there of their Constitutional rights, in the North, the de facto segregation still continued to raise its ugly head. African-Americans lived in the worst urban neighborhoods and attended the worst urban schools. The only positive thing in this legislation is that it ushered in a new era in which African-Americans could seek legal redress for civil rights violations. The Act, as noted by Lisa Vox not only led the way for the voting Rights but also paved the way for programs like affirmative action. [8]

The negative side of the law and indeed most other laws enacted to favor African-Americans since the end of the slavery in this country is that they still generate various forms of subtle servitudes including: racial, or ethnic, job, or employment, residential, gender discrimination, hate crime, stereotypes, and racial profiling. Racial profiling in particular generates many conflicts particularly between the police and the African-American young men who are sometimes killed at random by some of the Caucasian police officers. This subject is the main rationale for undertaking this write-up.

Chapter Two

Before delving into the racial profiling issues it is important to have an overview of racial discrimination.

What is Discrimination? By way of definition, discrimination is defined as a person or group treating another person or group negatively based on their race, nationality or solely on their membership in a socially distinct group or category such as race, nationality, gender, religion, age or disability. Although discrimination is found all over the world, we are going to limit our enquiry to the United States of America thereby miniaturizing what is seen in the entire global village. America is supposed to be a country where everyone is free. However, it is tainted by all sorts of racial discrimination particularly perpetuated by the majority Caucasians against minorities particularly African-Americans. Racial discrimination has become so engrained in the psyche of the nation so much that it continues destroying many lives on a daily bases. This is unfortunately perpetuated by some of those employed to safeguard lives and property- racist police officers. It also raises its ugly head within other sectors in society such as access to health care, educational services, employment opportunities, wage levels and criminal justice system, among others.

Unfortunately many victims of racial discrimination become racists themselves. Within the last forty years, the federal government has passed the following Acts and Commissions: Racial Discrimination in 1975; Gender Discrimination-1984; Human Rights and equal opportunity Commissions-1992; Disability Act- 1986; Equal Opportunity for women in work place-1996.

Superficial Cause of Racism

Superficial cause of racism is a difference in color pigmentation which is an inherited, physical characteristics that distinguishes one group from another. The arbitral anthropological definition of race recognizes three major racial divisions among human beings namely Caucasians(-Pale skinned people mostly from Europe); Mongolians(- yellow skinned people from Asia), and Negroid(- dark or brown skinned people found mostly in Africa).

A more detailed categorization of the human beings based on their races was compiled by Johann Friedrich Blumenbach, a German anthropologist. In his 1795 edition of De Generis humani varietate native (On the Natural Variety of Mankind) divided homo sapiens into five distinct races based on their physical characteristics: the yellow race Mongolian race; the red American race; the brown Malayan race; the Black Ethiopian race and the "white" Caucasian race. Blumenbach made this based on the shape of the differing races' skulls, which is assumed by some to be their determining characteristics or phrenology. For Blumenbach, the size and angle of the forehead, the jawbone, teeth, eye sockets etc. were of paramount importance. Observing that the above components of the body-structure of his race resembled those of people found in the Caucasus mountain range running along Georgia's northern, he named them Caucasians.

However it has been pointed out that while he categorized races, Blumenbach never put them in any hierarchy and protested any attempt to misuse his groupings to divide people or paint one group as inferior to another. He wrote forcefully of the kindness of human races and opposed the stress on racial hierarchies by his most conservative colleagues both in his university and elsewhere in Europe. His stance on this has been substantiated by historian Nell Irvin Painter who indicates that Blumenbach had been emphasizing the unity of mankind as well as opposing racial hierarchy. The synonymous usage of "Caucasian whites" as well as racial lines as discriminatory tools came later from others who were apparently suffering from an inferiority complex.

It is worth pointing out here that, as indicated above, the categorization of different races has no scientific connotation. America is a melting pot of all nationalities: it is supposed to be a nation where everybody, irrespective of his or her race is at home with others. It is historically a virgin land where people from every race and nationality came to make a living. In other words being an immigrant country America should be a country where diversity is celebrated since it is composed of people from every ethnic, cultural, racial and religious backgrounds. Yet throughout its history, whenever the country takes one step forward towards universal acceptance of all races via various regulations, the racists within the country push it two steps back through racial discrimination, profiling and murdering.

Causes of Racism

One of the reasons thought to be responsible for racism is the purported racial superiority of the Caucasians who call themselves "whites" over the African-Americans whom they call "Blacks". At this juncture we have to delve into various colors or complexions to discover in the first place whether there is any set of human beings created and endowed with a truly white or black complexion. I recall, when I was a young priest in 1986 studying in Rome. I took a summer vacation to Germany to learn German language in order to deepen my comprehension of theological courses since many of the theological books were written originally in German. Following the six weeks intensive course, I opted to assist in a German parish to improve on its spoken form for some weeks. It happened that within the period, the pastor had hired some locals to work on the rectory in which lunch was served along with some white and black colored deserts. In an attempt to make fun of my brown complexion, he asked that the black desert be passed on to me since it tallied with my color while they would go for the white colored desert. As if I did not know what he was alluding to, I asked why that particular color of the desert would have to be passed on to me. In reply- and to the laugher of everyone at the table- he said that I should eat the black colored dessert since that fitted well with my complexion, while the rest of them should go for the white colored one that went with theirs.

At this point I began a Socratic sort of questioning on whether or not children in the country were taught the difference between various colors. When he indicated that the children learned that in kinder-garden, I further asked whether they had a law in the country that would cause adults to forget the various colors they learnt while growing up. They probably were of the opinion that since I was learning the language I was not sure of what I intended to say, because I asked the pastor what colors his trousers and shirt he was wearing at the time were. He replied rightly, indicating that while his pair of trousers was black, the shirt was white. I then took him off-guard when I asked whether his pale complexion was the same as the color of his white shirt and whether my brown complexion was same as the color of the black dissert or his black trousers. He could not answer the question and everybody finished his meal in an unplanned silence. The advantage of the incident was that throughout the remaining period I spent with him, no further prejudiced word or remark ever came from his mouth.

One understood that in the past, when the world was viewed only from the white and black lenses depicting the strength of technology, two colors were shown on the television screens at the time. This would have caused some people to be focused on division between "black" and "white" people. Even this could never have made reasonable people, who would have been taught different colors, be so short-sighted to come to the level of calling almost everyone from Africa "Black" instead of brown and those from Europe" whites" instead of pales. Normal people know very well that, just as there are variations regarding colors in creation manifesting its beauty, what matters more than the color is the substance of someone or something.

Though individuals may prefer one specific color from an aesthetic or an individual aesthetic point of view, it is obvious that no single color is better than the other. The same is true of different sizes, heights and shapes or figures created and laid out in the world by the supreme designer or creator (God). In other words no person in his/her right mind would ever waste his time or other peoples' time harping on such an irrelevant thing as the complexion or color of his fellow human being since in the first place the individual was created so by the creator who does not need to consult anyone before creation. When he had finished creation, the creator saw that it "was good" – the people continue to be good provided no one tries disfiguring them via undue criticism of this beauty of creation. Some people attribute these attacks to a superiority complex which is really nothing other than a front, shielding a rather profound psychological inferiority complex. This superiority complex requires a more detailed examination.

John Osom, MSP

Superior Pigmentation and Mental Inferiority Complex

Many of those who feel that their color is superior do not admit that they themselves are colored or pigmented. This is the main rationale behind referring only to those from Africa or African-Americans, in particular, as colored people. However, common sense detects that no creature is colorless, otherwise how on earth would such a being be perceived? He would have been a spirit that cannot be seen. Those who claim to be "white", therefore admit to having white color, which implies that, they are colored, too. Princeton's WordNet, which attempts to make a distinction between colored and non-colored people, describes people of color as "a race with a skin pigmentation different from white race {especially blacks)"[1]. In its glossary attempt to make the distinction, he inevitably creates more confusion than clarification. When Luke Visconti, an acclaimed national recognized leader in diversity management, was asked whether "people of color" was the right terminology to describe a diverse population, (referring to those of African extraction) he replied that in his opinion, "people of color" is an effective way to describe a non- white people in the United States. According to him, to avoid endless semantics, it is more useful to use a common phrase to describe people who are commonly thought of as not being whites by the white majority in this country.

For Luke Visconti, 'people of color' is a respectful sounding phrase [2]. Obviously this so called expert sounds foolish before an average person except when he says "Ultimately I think we must all recognize that the conversation revolves around imaginary differences. There is only one human race and we are all originally from Africa. That's not a concept that the majority gives into easily."[3] Heating the nail on head, he says that when the bigots figure out the code, they are going to denigrate the word, log rolling themselves into irrelevance. In other words, imagine the 'wisdom' they pride themselves on by arrogating to themselves the "white" color (that no human being is ever endowed with) just to make themselves superior to the "blacks or colored people" they consider inferior. It should be noted, however, that the term 'colored people' was first used in South Africa to refer to those with mixed ancestry and so has a connotation different from the "people of color" intended as a slur discussed here.

According to Oxford advanced learner's Dictionary, the word pigment is defined as "a substance that exits naturally in people, animals and plants and gives their skins, leaves, etc, a particular color" [4] Pigmentation is defined as "the presence of pigments in the skin, hair, and so on that causes it to be of a particular color". This definition of pigment or pigmentation does not exclude any human being, animal or plant. So it simply implies that every human being or thing is necessarily pigmented or colored, otherwise it would not be a real substance nor would it have the ability to be labelled. The next step is to examine the different colors to be sure that everyone is on the same page when communicating what is in one's mind to an audience.

From the kinder-garden children all over the globe are taught the different colors and their respective names in their own language. It is expected that as we grow up, we will remember these differences, otherwise we will cause confusion when communicating. It is worth noting that the only beings that have no color are angels, God and spirits (including saints) and this is why they are never visible. While it might be tolerable for children in some countries to be told that their parents' dish is the most delicious in the whole world in order to enable them to develop an appetite for their mother's kitchen, it is absolutely ridiculous for someone to think that his complexion is superior to others'. That would indicate an infantile thought or a rather serious psychological derangement requiring immediate hospitalization. This attitude might have been as a result of unresolved psychological issues causing the individual to project his complexion as superior to feel better about himself while at the same time blocking himself from a particular imbalance within his psyche.

As if mere thought was not serious enough for medical attention, it is brought up into the open as a basis for dealing with fellow human beings whose God-given complexion is different. On the other hand, those who are deceived like children deceived into believing that their complexion is "inferior" are equally in the same shoes, since they are like these projectors in their infantile thoughts and words. I can still recall, when I was a child, how my senior siblings made me cry one day when they told me that, since I had mistakenly swallowed one of the seeds of an orange while sucking it, the seed would grow and transform me into an orange tree. When my mother returned and saw me crying, she not only consoled me with gifts- assuring me that the orange seed was going to be expelled from my system when using the rest room- but also cautioned my siblings against such a deceit. As already indicated what matters in life is never one's color or complexion but the moral or ethical integrity of the individual concerned. As Martin Luther King, Jr. rightly highlights, what makes an individual is not the color of the skin but rather the content of his character. "I have a dream that my four little children will one day be living in a nation where they will not be judged by the color of their skin but by the content of their character"[5].

As long as humans are still living in this global village, it is and will remain clear that just as no reasonable person attaches importance to the color of any material but rather its quality, no sane person attaches any importance to the skin color of any individual but rather the character of the person in question. In other words descriptive words or adjectives like one's shape, height, food, income etc, never define an individual; what matters is his or her character. To relate with someone on the basis of one's complexion or suspect someone of being a criminal on the basis of complexion is a disservice to any nation. Why would some people equate human complexion with a moral categorization, where the so called "white" is equated with good (and so must be cherished) while the "black" is an evil that must be rejected? In other words what sort of plague came on some Americans that they began to associate "white" with superiority, making it preferable to "black" as an inferior complexion that can only at best be tolerated, at worst dumped into a trash bin? These errors in their minds have been responsible for their mental and physical altering or falsification of brown into black and pale into white colors. Little do these people know that this is causing a great confusion in the minds of children, who are taught the distinction between one color from the other in the nursery school. Besides this, what comes across in this falsehood is "I am white and therefore good, trustworthy and superior to you blacks, who are not only inferior but also untrustworthy and therefore bad". Consequently, whatever is done by a "white" person is good and acceptable, while at the same time, whenever a "black ' person does the same thing, it has to be bad and consequently condemnable. In the minds of these people suffering from superiority complexes, all other complexions are inferior to theirs and so consequently must be at their beck and call.

This is the rationale behind some Caucasians in this category associating African-Americans with servile occupation. In the wake of protests in different cities following the racial police killing of African-Americans, president Barack and the first lady, Mrs. Michelle Obama shared their own stories of racial biases with People magazine during a recent interview. According to Michelle, "As a black man living in Chicago, Barack had his share of trouble catching cabs". She recalled a particular occasion when her husband, who was wearing a tuxedo and a black tie for dinner, was asked by someone- obviously a

Caucasian- to bring him a cup of coffee. The president himself said he was often mistaken for a valet for no other reason than the color of his skin. "There is no black male my age, who's a professional, who hasn't come out of the restaurant and waiting for his car and somebody didn't hand them their car keys" [6].

On her part, Michelle described how she was mistreated at a Target store during a suburban Washington shopping trip she took in 2011. "Even as the first lady", she told the Magazine, "during the wonderful publicized trip I took to Target ..the only person who came to me in the store was a woman who asked me to help her take something off a shelf ". According to her these incidents are regular course of life for African-Americans and a challenge for the country to overcome.[7]

During her speech to the 2015 graduating class at the university of Tuskegee, Mrs. Michelle Obama expressed different forms of racists remarks she experienced, even as first lady, and how she has developed a moral compass which prevents her from distraction by such remarks. She called on the students to be equally focused and to never allow racism to distract them from their goals in life. She said "The road ahead is not going to be easy. It never is, especially for folks like you and me. Because while we've come so far, the truth is those age-old problems are stubborn, and they haven't fully gone away"[8].

The age-old problems in question are obviously the problems of racism and the resultant discrimination that is the order of the day in America. She cited the recent police killing of African-Americans in Ferguson and Baltimore as some of the slights that every African American--- including her husband, the president and herself -are living with on a daily basis. Pinpointing a particular occasion of such slights, she recalls "The people at formal events who assumed that we were the "help"-and those who have questioned our intelligence, our honesty and even our love for this country". However despite this she urged the students to soar to their future, indicating that the past provided a blueprint for a country still struggling with the age-old problems of discrimination and race. [9].

Jim Grimsley— Caucasian—wrote an article published February23rd 2016, which not only backs up Michelle's position, but explains a more detailed manifestation of racism. Having already written a memoir detailing his own personal experience of racism among his fellow Caucasians, Grimsley asserts that whether one admits it or not, racism has become part of the DNA of every Caucasian. He recalls some years ago, following a church service hearing a deacon telling another deacon that "if God had meant white people and black people to mix, he would have made them one color". Grimsley added that the claim in question was made despite the Civil Rights demonstrations that were going on at the time in their home state of North Carolina as well as across the entire country amidst violent and non-violent protests. Having taken part in many discussions from the dismantling of Jim Crow laws until now, he is all too aware that progress on racial issues had hardly moved forward, adding that "white people are nearly as blind to their racism as ever"[10]

Grimsley gives an example of a lady who, in the course of their conversation affirmed her awareness of being raised in prejudice about African-Americans. However, as she grew up, she discovered, to her surprise that many of African-Americans, were as decent as some of her fellow Caucasians, contrary to what she was told when being raised. Grimsley then affirms:

"More than simple anecdotes, these are symptoms of the insanity of white culture and our refusal to understand that racism is part of our make up-- each and every one of us, north, south, east and west—from cradle to grave. We re-segregate our school using every available strategy and continue to profit from long—standing systems that biased towards the hiring, advancement and empowerment of white people, all the while decrying the racism we see in others, pointing fingers at this or that as if by saying, 'that one is a racist. "We exonerate ourselves of the charge" [11]

He admits to being one of the white liberals, adept at using naming or shaming tactics to avoid looking inward. "comfortable in our beliefs", he continues. "we ignore the fact that we sit inside an ideology of white superiority that gives us enormous advantages even when we mouth the right opinions, trade memes about awful racist act that one of us committed and pat ourselves on the back for our sensitivity". [12]. Being aware that they are in the minority, according to Jim, Caucasians embark on making movies, portraying everybody to be white, nominating white people to win all the best prizes pointing to the 2015th Oscar nominations as a practical example-- writing text books, and developing educational curricula that surround white heroes with halos and throw the achievement of other people into a ghostly relief. We set aside the month of February to pay oblige lip service to black history, but what that means for us white people is that we take a vacation from history, black history is for black people'. He rhetorically asks, aren't the racists the people who burn crosses and lynch black people?

Grimsley points out that, during a radio interview talk show, he asserted that a great deal of racism is unconscious and unintended. However, the host put him in his place when he asked, since the system of racism operates 24 hours a day,7 days a week without mercy or letup, affecting every single black person alive in our country, how could it possibly be unconscious? Finding no answer, Grimsley admitted he still failed to understand racism; even after decades of awareness, probing and trying to change on his part, it is still present in him and binding him to its reality [13].

This project is undertaken with a view to overcome this challenge, indicating first of all the genesis of this color or complexion misperception inherent in some Caucasians who unwittingly claim superiority of their pale complexion. They mistakenly proclaimed themselves "white", a color which the creator has not endowed on any human being.

Against the criticism that the president has not been aggressive enough in talking about issues of race and justice particularly in terms of African American men, he says "If you look at what happened with Michael Brown, if you look at what happened after Trayvon, if you look at the decision after Eric Garner, I 'm being pretty explicit about my concern, and being pretty explicit about the fact that this is a systemic problem that black folks and Latinos and others are not just making this up" [12].

Racial Profiling

Racial profiling is the invidious use of race or ethnicity as a criterion in conducting stops, searches and other investigative procedures by the law enforcement officers to criminalize people of a particular race. It is premised on the erroneous assumption that individuals of one particular race or ethnicity are more likely to engage in misconduct than individuals from another race or ethnicity. It goes without saying that racial profiling in law enforcement perpetuates negative racial stereotypes which are harmful to any country, especially to this country, which is rich and diverse despite materially impairing every effort to maintain a fair and just society.

Despite the unconstitutionality of racial profiling and the government declaration that the practice is unacceptable, racial profiling is still encouraged by misguided federal programs which incentivize law enforcement authorities to engage in the practice. This is reflected under "Hate Crime" which was defined by Congress in 1969 as a criminal offence against a person or property motivated in whole or in part by an offender's race, religion or ethnicity"[13]. This was expanded in 2009 to include disability and sexual orientation following a protracted lobbying by LGBT groups. In this federal crime statute, it is pointed out that if the local authorities decline to persecute a hate crime, the federal government can take over, making hate crime offenders more likely to face prosecution.

An important question to consider is this: how would racial profiling ever be faced if the police, the very people meant to protect people and uphold the law, are the ones perpetuating this practice? This was spelled out by Wade Henderson, the president of the leadership conference, when he observed that since the guidance issued by John Ashcroft- the attorney General in 2003- did not apply to state or local government police, how likely would federal agents engage in routine law enforcement activities such as traffic and pedestrian stops? According to the memoranda circulated by the U.S. senior law enforcement officials worldwide in 2002, it is clear that race is considered an effective measure of an individual's intent to commit a crime. Isn't it a waste of resources when the offices concerned ignore actual suspicious behavior of someone who does not fit into a racial profile, thereby encouraging the crimes officers are paid to prevent?

Chapter Three

Kingdom divided against itself heading towards doom (Mtt.12:25-26)

Statistically, it is estimated that 70% of both African American and Latino students get expelled from school annually. A new study examining unconscious biases against African-Americans in the school system explains why racial tensions run high in communities like Baltimore even where many of those in position of power are African-Americans. In two strikes: Race and Disciplining of young students, Stanford psychologists, Jennifer Eberhard and Jason Okonofua try figuring out the reason as to why African American students are punished more harshly by teachers than their Caucasian counterparts. The two psychologists suspect racial stereotypes contribute to how harshly students' behavior are judged and how teachers interact with them. From their research they conclude that generations of anti-black sentiments and negative portrayals of African-Americans in the media have caused many to internalize stereotypes about African-Americans which invariably trickles into the classroom[1].

Like police officers, African American teachers in public schools are part of the system that has a long history of institutionalized discrimination. According to Melinda D. Anderson, a D.C based education writer and parent's activist, "white means right and black means lack"[2].

From what is said above, it is unfortunate that a few African-Americans themselves are so traumatized that they regard their God-given brown complexion as being inferior to that of their Caucasian or pale -complexioned counterparts. Otherwise what on earth would have made them to be part of the ban-wagon meting-out more punishment to African American students than their Caucasian counterparts?

On the other hand, could it be that the African-Americans teachers' disciplinary behavior towards their same complexion students are misinterpreted by the researchers? Further research needs to be done to really ascertain whether the actions taken by the African American teachers stem from bias or from a desire to inculcate discipline into the students, most of whom are from single parent families. Since children from single families have no fathers living with them, the working mothers have no time to instill some discipline the students need to graduate from school.

If on the other hand, the research is authenticated, in the sense of the teachers embarking on punishing the children out of bias, it would simply imply that, they are a kingdom divided against itself that is doomed to fail. In other words the teachers would be supporting the assertion of Melinda Anderson cited above. Should that be the case, then the African American teachers themselves would be "lacking" which implies that they themselves have nothing to offer, since nothing implied in "lacking" cannot offer anything.

A little more analysis of the white being "right and black lacking" needs to be made here. There is an adage to the effect that what is a mistake in England, is a fashion in Africa. The two countries are named here simply because of the fact that England whose colonies were America and most countries in Africa certainly have a common experience of the latter's colonization. From the analysis of the encounter of the immigrants from Britain down here to what was then known as the new world, America, it is known that no sooner they were received warmly by the Native Americans than the immigrating Britons availed of their superior weapons and subdued their hosts and turned them into slaves. This was prior to the arrival of Africans captured and taken into this country as slaves by some of the same Britons though their enslavement was worse than those of the Native Americans.

It must have been the ability to secure superior weapons that made the Caucasians arrogate to their complexion a rather false superiority complex. This would obviously be the same time when they stated falsifying their true complexion from pale to white. Simultaneously the Caucasians started looking down on the complexion of the African-Americans by falsely ascribing blackness to their brown complexion. Besides this since the Caucasians were using the knowledge of their weapons, as already indicated, to traumatize other races, they succeeded in exploiting their resources which was what colonization in the first place was all about. They enriched themselves while those they exploited become more empoverished. On the basis of this sort of exploitation, they gradually built up the obnoxious notion that "whatever a white man says or does is right while at the same time whatever a black man says or does is nothing". Since one is generally identified with his home country or place of birth, the already indicated adage was formulated warning every African to desist from copying the Caucasians blindly. Africans were warned against taking as a norm the exploitation of their fellow Africans as was done by the Britons during their colonization era which, in the first place, was morally wrong. The warning is not only restricted to the past but also, more than ever, now repeated due to the rather obnoxious practice of legalized homosexuality which has become a norm in the western world. This is, of course, greatly resisted by most African countries based on the elementary physics' principle that like poles dispel while unlike poles attract.

Manipulation of one's complexion or an outright deceit on one's complexion for undue advantage

Some people have made themselves so unsatisfied with their God-given nature that they are now feigning their gender as well as the color of their skin for some ulterior motives. Some of them, created and born males, undergo surgery purporting to transform themselves into women and vice versa on one hand, while on the other hand, some born "black" turn "white" and recently a Caucasian claims that she is "black". Reported by Andriana Diaz who interviewed the clamant, Rachel Dolezal, on June 12th,2015, was accused of falsely portraying herself as a black woman. However when her parents were interviewed they pointed out that she was misrepresenting "major portions of her life" including being born white". While being interviewed, Rachel said "Actually I don't like the term African-American; I prefer black,… So if asked, I would say yes, I consider myself to be black"[3]

As indicated above, when interviewed, her biological parents deny her allegation. Her mother, Ruthanne, says "Our daughter is primarily German and Czech and European descent…Rachel has wanted to be somebody she's not. She's chosen not to just be herself but to represent herself as an African-American woman or a biracial person. [4]

One can, however, be led to the conclusion that ultimately Rachel technically arrives from her scholarly research focused on the intersection of race, gender and class in contemporary Diaspora with specific emphasis on black woman, visual culture, the evolutional origins of human life indicating that we are all from African continent. One's mother land is very essential and so if Africa is the mother land of all other nations, Rachel, going further to call herself a black woman may not be entirely or scholarly disproved.

Though her parents, Lawrence and Ruthanne Dolezal, a Caucasian couple from Montana, quoted as saying that while they see nothing wrong with their daughter advocating for African-American rights, they do not think that she should deceive anyone about her own ethnic background which is, according to them, German and Czech. However both the parents and their daughter are affirming the same thing but at two different levels. Obviously on her ethnicity, which is according to her, "a multilayered issue" and this is affirmed by her parents as German and Czech. But with regards to her origin, while the parents are focusing on their immediate origin, she, based on her research, focusses on the ultimate origin of everyone. This is confirmed when she said "We're all from the African continent". Knowing very well that not many people have any historical knowledge of the origin of different races in the world, when questioned she said: "The question is not as easy as it seems. There are a lot of complexities …and I don't know that everyone will understand that". [5] Her identification with African-Americans may be one of the ways towards building cultural gaps by indicating that we are all humans regardless of skin color. However her motive for pretending to be black is simply in order to keep her job of not only being taken seriously as a professor of African culture, but also as a leader of the NAACP,(National Association for the Advancement of Colored People), along with being the chairperson of the police over sight committee. She had to quit these positions a couple of days following the uproar from her false ethnicity claim. This is a complete simulation of her research which she has taken an undue advantage of. The sight of Rachel as a bundle of contradiction is further manifested when she told Matt Lauer during an interview: "I was drawing self-portraits with the brown crayon instead of peach crayon". She is known to have African American step-siblings, attended a historically an African American university, Howard where she graduated in 2002. This was the year she filed a lawsuit against Howard claiming that she was denied a scholarship and teaching post for being Caucasian, a suit dismissed in 2004. Rachel got married to an African-American with two children before she got divorced. All these factor into the area of self-contradiction especially when she affirmed "I am more black than white". She describes herself as bisexual dating men and women. From the above analysis it is obvious that Rachel is a person of split identity, a person simultaneously wanting to eat her cake and have it.

Notwithstanding pressure from different angles, from her research, she should have been systematic in her identification with the continent of Africa from where every other continent emanated without having to necessarily deny her Caucasian birth. In other words as rightly noted by Abdul-Jabbar in an online column in Time Magazine, "You can't deny that Dolezal has proven herself a fierce and unrelenting champion for African-Americans politically and culturally. Perhaps some of this sensitivity comes (sic) from her adoptive black siblings. Whatever the reason, she has been fighting the fight for several years and seemingly doing a first rate job. Not only has she led her local chapter of the NAACP, she teaches classes related to African-Americans culture at Eastern Washington and is chairwoman of the police over-sight committee monitoring fairness in police activities. The black community is better off because of her."[7]

On the other hand, Blair L. M. Kelley points out that "race is social construct. But that it isn't real as a lived experience in America. And it wasn't constructed out of the thin air. On this broken American foundation, African-Americans led, created communities and built a movement that transformed, and strives to further transform America for the better. It may have been good for Dolezal to play as an ally in that movement if she had pursued it but not as a white woman masquerading as a black woman".[8] Commenting on the incident, Freund Thomas says that the deception is problematic because people don't choose their race. "Dolezal is probably benefiting from her African American identity without having experienced a life time of racism, and she can shed her black persona if it becomes inconvenient. She can hide in her whiteness at any moment if she wants to". The main issue here is that racial identification does exist in some ahistorical bubble of self- determination as Churis Jones indicates when making reference to Rachel Dolezal. [9]

An African American, not pleased with the incident, expressed his view to Rolling Stone: "You cannot just jump back and forth between these two worlds. It is very disrespectful of people of color that she claims to identify with to say something like that. When you say something like that, you are not identifying with us, at all, in any way, shape or form" [10].

Some days later, the following African-Americans weighed in on the self-deceit of Rachel Dolezal: (i) Tara Setmayer, in her article titled: "Why the fascination with Rachel Dolezal"?, expresses her anger over lionizing a liar, pointing out that in today's world anybody just feels free to turn things upside down. This, according to her, is what is happening in the bizarre world of Rachel Doleza. Simply because she says so, is prompting many to be debating on all sides of her deceptive behavior. From all indications, she seems, rationalizing the absurd has become a pastime of the left. "Rachel is a liar creating a complex world of delusion she perpetuated for years, wondering whether the delusion stems from Caucasian guilt of 'nth' degree or some other pathology. It is dangerous to lionize a liar raising a question as to whether integrity even matters any longer when one is ideologically aligned". [11]

Tara further points out that the mentality of 'anything goes, because I feel like it', is a recipe for disorder in a civil society. She rhetorically asks where the line can be drawn in a world where absolute truth no longer exists before the Rachel Dolezals of the world become a new norm.[12]

(ii) Jeff Yang, in an article titled: "Who really has white privilege"?. maintains that: "For some white Americans, Dolezal is a validation of highly suspect notion that melanin is a social advantage and that minorities now have access to privileges that Caucasian counterparts do not". She contends that Rachel is an example of how white entitlement extends just about every aspect of life in America, how it shrouds even the ability to determine the bounds of one's own culture and community rather than have it defined by the whims of others.[13]

(iii) Jess Row thinks that Rachel is gripping America because some Americans are taking the moment to consider the absurdity, arbitrariness and psychological violence of racism. According to Jess, one thing about understanding racism is that it makes us shy away from complexity, from awkwardness, from the sight of a white mother with black children, from questions like: "Where did you get her or where are you really from"? The truth, according to Jess, is that we are all related and subject to our own strange, interwoven desires. Perhaps by encountering this story of deception and denials, one becomes more comfortable with not hiding from one another, the best possible outcome.

(iv) Sophia Nelson says that Rachel's deceit is grating on her nerves so badly as a black woman, because she represents hundred of years of African American women being invisible and the Caucasian women being heard. Comparing this to the tale of a white female rescuing black women from danger, Sophia says "The black women's voices are muted while the white women voices are not".[14] She indicates that white and black women had been having complicated relationship dating back to slavery through Jim Crow era when they (i.e. African American women) worked as maids to white women. And up to the present day African American women are serving as managers and protégées of white women.

Consequently when they see Rachel with her kinky hair and fake bronze skin, it shakes them to the sore. According to Sophia, this sort of cheap imitation is both an insult and injury for many of them (African American women) on the national and global TV platform. This is giving force to their black experience yet, real black women are often tossed about like a political football when it suits others to climb their backs so that they can stand up. "If a white woman pretends to be one of us and is given a chance to speak for us, and our experiences as a black woman, what do we have left? In a world that stereotypes us as angry, local, too much of this, not enough of that, Rachel Dolezal proves once again that we still don't exist". [15].

(v) Michaela Angela Davis is annoyed with Rachel not only because real blacks live with relentless threat of violence and death, but also sort to take their actual stories, their stories of resistance and survival. She rhetorically asks: "When black women like Renisha McBride got killed, how can a white person claim to "own" black experience"?[16]

(vi) Dean Obeidallah, in her article titled: "Will controversy change things"?, wonders whether Rachel is delusional. The real question is will Rachel's story bridge the racial divide or better understand the social construct of identity"? [17]

One thing that clearly stands out from the various utterances of African-Americans outlined above, is that non-withstanding Rachel's attempt to identify with African-Americans, from the knowledge of her research work as well as growing up with her

African American adopted siblings, she shouldn't have claimed to speak in this context as a "black" woman since experience (of which she cannot personally acquire) speaks louder than words if ever she was sincere.

An eye for an eye & a tooth for a tooth reaction against police brutality complicates rather than solves the problem

Quoting from Lev. 24:17. In which revenge was tolerated, Jesus Christ, the teacher, in Matthew's Gospel (Mtt. 5,38) explains that returning evil for evil complicates rather than solves any problem at stake. Besides this we are aware of the dictum according to which two evils never make a right. If it is not right to unnecessarily take laws into one's hands on the part of the police officer who harms or kills a fellow human being based on the ground of the victim's complexion, how much more can one contemplate engaging one's self in murdering innocent police officers on their difficult tasks of protecting the communities under their care? Anyone who cares, knows that besides being so difficult a task, policing any community hardly wins sympathetic or appreciation from those protected. This is well summed up by the Dallas police chief, David Brown when, in the wake of Dallas killing of five police officers and wounding of seven others in the course of protecting the protesters over the police killings of two African-Americans in Baton Rouge and Minnesota, said: "Cops don't expect to hear the words, 'thank you', very often especially from those who need them most". [18] Within five days following the memorial service of the five police officers, three other police officers were shot dead and others wounded in Baton Rouge.

President Barack Obama at the Dallas Memorial pointed out that the police never make laws but rather do the harder part by ensuring the maintenance of the laws on daily basis to uphold the constitutional rights of the people exercising their right when engaging in the protest referred to above. The senseless murder by the demented man prompted by racial hatred, according to the President, presents America as if the deepest fault lines of her democracy have suddenly been exposed perhaps even widened. He says "We wonder if an African American community that feels unfairly targeted by police, and police Departments that feel unfairly maligned for doing their jobs can ever understand each other's experience". [19] According to him, sometimes it is hard not to think that the center will not work. The president, however, pointed out that America is not as divided as it may seem. Even among the Caucasians, not everyone of them was apparently pleased at the killing of the two African-Americans. This is shown by the presence of a good number of the Caucasians at the protest marches that took place in many states within the country. Shetamia Taylor, one of those shot trying to shield her two boys during the protest, was cited as saying that she wanted her boys to join her protest the incidents of black men being killed.

The President highlighted that working together as a nation with one destiny has already been manifested by both the Major, a Caucasian and the Police chief, an African American. Consequently within a short time, apart from reducing the crime rates in Dallas, the rate of murder has been reduced by sixty four percent. This was intended to show that Caucasians and African-Americans along with other minorities can work peacefully together if they open their hearts to one another through authentic dialogue. This entails respect and equal treatment of everyone in the country.

As will be highlighted in the next chapter, an overwhelming majority of the Caucasian Police officers do an incredibly hard and dangerous job fairly and professionally, President Obama commended them as deserving of our honor and not our scorn. He highlighted that those who resort to rhetoric suggesting harm to police officers, even if they do not act on it themselves, do not only make the jobs of police officers even more dangerous but also do a disservice to the very course of justice that they claim to promote.

Reference to Century of Racial Discrimination-of Slavery and Subjugation, and Jim Crow.

President Obama, in his Dallas Memorial Address analysed above, also pointed out some sore points in the national life that did not simply vanish with the law banning segregation, or with Dr. Martin King Jr's speech or when voting Right Acts were signed. Race relations have greatly improved, a denial of this fact is dishonoring the struggles that helped in achieving the progress. However, the President says: "it is well known that bias still remains." Bias and bigotry are seen across board—"black or white or Hispanic or Native Americans or Middle Eastern descent have personally experienced this monster, bigotry in life at some point. While some suffer far more under racism's burden, some feel discrimination sting. Although some do their best to guard against it and teach their children better, non is entirely innocent." Since no institution is entirely immune, police department is included as it is well known. Heating the nail on the head he says: "And so when African-Americans from all works of life, from different communities across the country voice a growing despair over what they perceived to be unequal treatment... When study after study shows that whites and people of color experience the criminal justice system differently, so that if you're black, you're more likely to be pulled over or searched or arrested, more likely to get longer sentences, more likely to get the death penalty for same crime; when mothers and fathers raised their kids right and have the talk about how to respond if stopped by a police officer...yes sir...no sir, but still fear that something terrible may happen when their child walks out the door, still fear that kids being stupid and not quite doing things right might end in tragedy... When all this took place more than fifty years ago after the passage of the civil Right Acts, we cannot simply turn away and dismiss those in peaceful protest as trouble makers or paranoid. We can't simply dismiss it as symptom of political correctness or reverse racism. To have your experience denied like that, dismissed by those in authority, dismissed even perhaps by your white friends and co-workers and fellow church members. Again and again and again- it hurts".[20]

It has to be emphasized that the above long passage from the recent speech of the President of this country is quoted here simply because it summarizes some of the contents of this book.

Charring Ball says that "Racism' is systematic and continues in order to ensure that groups outside the dominant culture, particularly African-Americans cannot rise to the same level of equality, justice and freedom as our white counterparts. She also points out that the first lady, Michelle Obama, has gradually abandoned her effort to pass legislation which would have made healthier food more accessible: "And no matter how much personal wealth and status one can acquire within the confines of this system or how many of us become Doctors., nurses, lawyers and even presidents of the United States, we are still going to be treated and regarded as inferior. And if the neutralization of Michelle Obama is not enough proof of that, then consider how Barack, her husband, has been politically neutered because of his race including constantly being maligned and undermined in the halls of Congress and not being able to speak and act freely on the issue of police brutality possibly, out of fear of what the dominant culture will say and do to him. But by not telling the next generation of us the truth about this country, we are ultimately saying to our youth that their places, as second-class citizens in their own land of birth is okay. That they should accept their positions and work within the parameters set by the majority". [21]

This remark would be rather discouraging if Charing Ball did not also see the need for perseverance, which has always been the rationale for Barack, the first African-American elected president of the United States. In her closing sentence, Charing Ball says :" That kind of mindset breeds complacency when what we actually need are change makers"[22].

Indeed, President Barack Obama campaign's slogan "Change" has started bearing fruits for America, starting with the change from a Caucasian to African-American Presidency. However, one's ability to get things done, to influence, to exercise authority, and to bring one's environment under control has an enormous influence on how secured one feels in his ability to keep himself safe as well as his ability to get what he wants and do the sort of things he wants to see accomplished. As observed by Howard Ross, there are different ways that this kind of power can be manifested in both organizational and personal life. Coercive power is within this particular area of this enquiry. Before applying it to the subject of our investigation, it is important to briefly examine what it is.

Coercive power is the ability to use positional force or dominance to get people to comply to one's desire, as a result of positioning someone in a formal structure within an organization. Coercive power can manifest itself in both positive and negative ways. Used negatively, coercive power causes one, to fear danger in defying an authority figure. Police officers on the road belong to this category of authority. This explains why commuters have to obey them on the road. Some Caucasian police officers take undue advantage of the minorities, like the African-Americans. Many a time, this powerlessness is displayed interpersonally when interacting with others. It can be a function, as Howard observes, of being with people, exhibited in the way one behaves or the language he uses. Besides this, various structures and systematic rules, policies and procedures and even one's language can unwittingly reinforce the dynamics of power.

Just as one of the negative sides of power is discrimination or negative bias, its positive side is privilege, which is a special advantage, immunity or benefit enjoyed only by some people in a community. Like power, privilege in general manifests itself on the personal, interpersonal and at institutional levels and is characterized in many ways. In general, privileges are often characterized as legitimate or not depending on whether or not they are clearly spelled out and relate to clear conditions. However very often, privilege is far more subtle and has unclear roots which is the main reason why it is discussed here. As Howard Ross points out, dominant group can often be the source of hidden privilege, which may never outwardly appear as hurtful to others who never benefit from it. It may be so pervasive and invisible when its benefit is gotten. It appears as something earned thus giving its beneficiaries the impression that others can equally have the same provided they work hard or employ similar algorithm [23]. Members of this dominant group consequently are not even aware that they are having a rather unmerited favors. It is this lack of an awareness which prevents or blinds them from seeing the presence of power and privileges they enjoy even if it is obvious to those outside the dominant group. This concealing of power and privilege, as observed by Howards Ross, is exacerbated by the fact that bias is looked at with the assumption of intent. Due to the fact that bias is thought as a function of overt act of bigotry, one remains blind to the invisible structure, systems, and behaviors that bestow and reinforce the power and privilege on a daily basis [24].

It is this dynamics that is playing itself out in some of the Caucasian police officers on the road. Following the fact that dominant group members often have assumed motive and react accordingly, they become rather defensive when confronted with behavior that they are not even aware that they are engaging in. This, to some extent, might explain the strand of some of the police officers and many a grand attorney that normally exculpates the officers when they unduly get the minorities shot on the roads. Some of the Caucasian police officers, relying on their unearned skin privilege, are conditioned to oblivion regarding its existence. These Caucasian police officers take undue advantage of the poor African-Americans by either killing them or sending them to prison with whatever false accusation they level against the victims. From the fore-going reflection on the dynamics, it becomes obvious that power, like other forms of biases, is a blind spot that is easily noticed by others apart from those exercising it.

In fact these complex networks of bias surrounding us daily make a profound impact on life of which one is very often unaware.

Apart from power, culture is another source of bias since it has a profound influence on our behavior and is equally unconscious for the most part. While it may seem relatively easy to correct a single act of unconscious bias as Howards Ross points out, it is almost impossible to notice how profoundly one is ensnared in the webs of instances in which bias affects our institutions [25]. There are three powerful ways in which culture affect our daily lives namely: legal system, Health- care and politics. A brief examination of each of these is necessary here.

(i)**The Legal System:** With a citation from the research done by Kelly Welch, Howard Ross points out the subtle and not so subtle messages that brand African-Americans "the criminal elements". It is compounded more by the media by identifying African-Americans particularly their young men as criminals [26]. Besides African-Americans, Hispanics are portrayed far more as criminals, drug users, sex workers and consequently less functional citizens. These are passed down to young children who internalize these stereotypes and the associated bias. On the part of the media, it contributes to this identification not only via fictionalized head-lines but also in reporting startling news which, in some cases, are out of context. These images, constantly associating African-Americans and Latinos with crimes, unconsciously link in the minds of many citizens, law enforcement officers on the road, lawyers, Judges and juries. As already highlighted earlier, this leads to much concentration on the part of some Caucasian police officers to the "stop and search" regulation aimed mostly at the African-Americans and Latinos in this country. The "stand your ground" laws enacted in many states are as, Howards points out, the brain behind the assassination of the young man, Trayvon Martin, Florida in 20012. Even the accused in the criminal justice or rather "injustice" system, more other areas of bias surface.

Assigning Low Cadre and Uncommitted Attorneys to the Poor Accused of Criminality

When assigning attorneys to those accused of criminality, rather low cadre of attorneys or public defenders who even if, on very rare cases, are deeply committed to the case may not have any resources to provide adequate defense for the poor African-Americans /Latinos to whom they are assigned. High cadre attorneys are reserved for Caucasians. From research, it is noted that biases in the court of law extend to some of those on trial. When asked to speak, the accent of those on trial are used by some judges in accessing either to dismiss a particular case or sentenced the alleged culprit to imprisonment. This is also true of the selection of juries as well for the juries themselves access the information of the alleged culprits in the court. Apart from the court, bias is manifested even among ex-convicts of same crime applying for the same job. They get employed or denied based on their races. As noted by authors, Devah, and his companions, black men are only one third as likely to get a positive response as their white counterparts, despite having identical qualifications and drug-related offences. Worst of all, newly released white felons often experience better job hunting success than young black men with no criminal record [27].

(ii) **The Health Care- System**: Generalized societal bias is much more affecting health care delivery. This is not only true in terms of access issues but also in the recognition that experiences of discrimination have been found to be a rather important type of psychosocial stressor leading to adverse changes in health status and altered behavioral patterns that increase health risks. The health-Care in question is not only to be assessed from the standpoint of treatment but also from its availability to the poor particularly the African-Americans and the Latinos who are low-income communities. Due to bias many practitioners never establish offices in the minority neighborhoods like those of African-Americans and Latinos. Besides this, many in these categories wouldn't, in the first place, have health insurance neither would the economically restricted have time to take off from work nor take their dependents for treatment. All these issues and many others, no doubt, make a profound impact on the overall health of any family suffering from the effect of bias. Even when someone is admitted into the hospital, many other factors based on bias are at the fore. Besides the patient's socio economic status, Language/accent and of course race, play a big role on how they are treated, how seriously their concerns are taken and how they are communicated with by the hospital staff as well as how students are treated by faculty members in medical schools.

(iii) **Politics**: Bias invades American politics in many ways. As noted by Howard Ross, the network of contention existing in our political structure creates dynamics on both sides of the political spectrum which is polarizing people and their political beliefs. The tectonic plates of American politics are shifting dramatically and the crevasses in the national politics are growing wider and deeper on a daily bases. Howard observes that the normal back and forth argument in politics for orienting the country towards the overall good of the nation is lacking. This cuts across journalism indicating that in the past there were very little political difference between journalists who were very focused on reporting unbiased news unlike now when the line between journalism and punditry has virtually disappeared. Consequently very few reporters nowadays are completely objective. We are now living in the world fueled by a media industry that is heavily rewarded for how much it responds to inflame partisan sentiments.

Allied to increased polarization is the rise of the mob on both sides of the political spectrum over the past several years. This has impacted the rise of "psychsclerosis", which according to Howard, does not only create self-righteousness but also an identification with their respective points of view, making those who differ with them appear as "others" or political enemies. As soon as that happens, the capacity for reasoning begins to decline since such decisions are not made by rational minds but profoundly influenced by emotions.[28] People then begin to have fixed views just as their political identities become more fixed and so as some approach political conventions, they would have already made up their minds to side with a political candidate irrespective of that candidate's view of things. This is in the same vein played out during elections when most people vote based on that fixated idea. The same study undertaken on the impact of bias on medical decision making, an issue contributing to the continuing patterns of health disparity negatively affecting African-Americans, Latinos, Native Americans, women etc., should be done for those who are already police officers.

Workshops or other learning modules that can help the cops learn non conscious processes providing them with skills aimed at reducing bias when interacting with African-Americans and other minorities should be undertaken. Such skills in practice include automatically bringing up discussion on egalitarian goals, searching for common identities and counter stereotypical information and embracing the perspectives of the minority.

Following many years of research in the field, Howard Ross identifies the following six major areas to which adequate attention should be paid:

(i) **Acknowledging Bias as a normal human experience**; every human being is, in one way or the other, biased and so denying it makes the matter worse since one cannot technically live without it. Once it is understood that bias is our fundamental survival mechanism, it will help everyone to bring compassion to others and of course to ourselves as well. To achieve this, one needs to discard the historic "good person /bad person" paradigm of diversity work and acknowledge that we are humans with all limitations in us. The human experience in us makes it clear that while we are at the forefront of kicking against people who manifest some disregard for who we are or choose to be, we nonetheless criticize others for their particular idiosyncrasy.

In other words everyone has some negative reaction to someone else. When someone believes that bias makes him a bad person, his mind moves either to self-recrimination, denial or self-justification, none of which moves him closer to being fully present to those with whom he interacts. It should be noted that making someone access a particular bias in him is not the same as condemning such individual. As it has already been highlighted, there is no human being without some biases and so what is of paramount importance is to help such a person to gradually become aware of it in order to neutralize it before being in a position of working towards its elimination. It is important not to treat people who don't know that they are demonstrating bias in a way suggesting that they are bad people. If that were to be the case they would not only be defensive but one loses the ability to influence them positively as well. The accused would not have any idea of what is at stake. When one turns himself from self-criticism on biases and is focused on self-exploration, he is on the way towards achieving the goal of this enquiry. This can be done since our ego is never permanent but constantly shifts and evolves, influenced by the narrative we are focused as well as the integration of the experiences we are encountering at a particular moment.

(11) **Developing the capacity for self-observation**; When we consciously observe ourselves, we have the opportunity of stepping on the clutch and neutralizing our biases by dis-identifying from the automatic reactions that normally dominate our thoughts. One can observe himself from different levels especially one's behavior, what he is saying and doing at a particular moment. The tools needed here are meditation and contemplation since they help in quieting the incessant chatter of the mind as well as bringing a sense of deeper tranquility and reflection. If one takes this sort of break in his thinking, he can disable the stress-bias reaction which helps him to be more present to what is going on within him on the spot. To achieve this, he has to develop another practice that is very important in navigating his unconscious bias via the creation of constructive uncertainty examined bellow.

(iii) **Practicing Constructive Uncertainty**; Culturally one is contented with what he thinks he is so certain about. This gets him into the wrong answer more than he would if he were to have taken much time to ruminate over the right one. Biases are generally fast, being that they are reflective reactions emanating from his limbic system. The automaticity of these responses makes someone to react to them without questioning. To proceed to a more conscious state, to start engaging in the prefrontal neocortex in metacognitive thinking, one needs to pause. As affirmed by Roll May "human freedom involves our capacity to pause between stimulus and response, and in that pause, to choose the one response towards which we want to through our weight. The capacity to create ourselves, based on this freedom, is inseparable from consciousness or self-awareness"[29].

When one observes himself he gets an opportunity to evaluate the circumstance in which he finds himself. By so doing, he is in a position to pay attention to what is happening beneath the judgment and assessment, acknowledge his reaction, interpretations and judgments. This enables him to understand other possible reactions, etc. that may be possible prior to searching for the most constructive, empowering or productive way of dealing with the situation.

Finally the action plan is executed. This is the stage in which constructive uncertainty leads to better thinking at which point one begins to turn ones exclamations into question marks and does not feel the need to be so sure of himself all the time. As Howard Ross points out, "the other benefit of constructive uncertainty is that it makes us far more opened to the ideas and perspective of other people"[30].

At this point one has to be skeptical without necessarily being cynical of what he thinks he knows with all amount of certainty in order to be helped to view things he might have missed in his certainty. It is necessary to make it clear that the afore mentioned subtitle, "Constructive Uncertainty" is intended to bring home to us that, a pause can be of immense help towards being more thoughtful and help disengage some of the automaticity of one's bias.

(1v). **Exploring awkwardness or Discomfort**: Exploring awkwardness or discomfort around certain kinds of people or certain circumstances is another way of working on one's personal biases especially when the people in question trigger some amount of misgiving within the individuals. Once one is having a strong emotional reaction stimulating some fear, this is a clear sign that one is reacting from his past. At this point one has to ask himself the following searching questions: Is the individual reacting to what is happening at the time? Is the situation currently threatening him? Is there any action that needs to be taken? How often do such people or situations affect him? Is there somebody with whom he could discuss the situation?

(v). **Engaging with people in groups one may not know very well or about whom one harbors biases**: As an Harvard psychologist, Gordon Allport, postulated, under the right circumstances, contact between conflicting groups is an effective way of diminishing prejudice and stereotyping. The more one gets to know people for who they are, the less he treats them like what they appear to him [31].

(vi) **Feedback and Data**; In order to get the sort of data and feedback needed in this venture, one has to find a way of creating an enabling environment around himself to make people willing to be engaged in the question.

The next area to which adequate attention must be paid is that of re-programming the status quo biases. A little comparison is warranted here. In the past, the orchestra musicians were overwhelmingly men before an awareness was created via women's movement of the 1960 and 1970s. This, no doubt, provided inspiration but specific changes came up when the evaluators were asked to evaluate the music rather than the physical appearance of the individual playing it. And as such, women were eventually recognized as musicians on their own right. In the same way when Caucasian Police officers interact regularly with the minorities, they can create community consciousness that can potentially help them live up to a higher standard demanded by their assignment. Fortunately as already pointed out earlier, since some of the Caucasian Police officers do their job without racial discrimination, the non- biased officers should liaise between their biased officers and the minority. Having the support of their fellow Caucasians will help the biased ones work towards discovering, admitting and consequently working towards the elimination of their biases. This can be achieved through a continuous engagement in the elimination of the biases in question while at the same time guiding against the inclination to slip into the old pattern. True cultural change occurs through long-term planning and sustainable action. I couldn't agree more with Howard Ross than his assertion that "once people have a fundamental understanding of bias, they can begin to expand their awareness by doing continuous personal exploration, looking at the ways they and their terms are functioning and installing some of the new organizational structures and system that can help reduce bias in the everyday process.

Unconscious bias education does not completely shift people's awareness, but it can be a powerful beginning for the process of shitting awareness. Most importantly, it can help people begin to shift their mind-set about how they handle their behavior within the system. All of the strategies in the world won't make any difference if you have never created a shift in mind-set". [32]

The in-ability to create a shift in the mind-set was, for example, clearly manifested in the June 8th, 2015 man-handling of Eric Casebolt, a Caucasian police officer now suspended, for brutally pinning to the ground an African American teenage girl and pointing out a gun on others at a pool party disturbance in McKinney, Texas. The incident occurred when teenagers were celebrating the end of the academic year party. The thirteen year old Jahda Bakari who did the videoing of the event said "I honestly believe it was about race because mostly they did nothing to the Caucasians". Highlighting the dilemma in which the children found themselves, one of the children reported how the police officer was trying to get them out of the play-ground: "... but if we ran, they chase after us, and if we stayed, then they arrest us"[33]. The video indicated the officer, Eric Casebolt, chasing the boys and cursing them as he pulled them to the ground.

Chapter Four

Proposals Towards Minimizing Racial Discrimination

Before delving into the intricacy of why some Caucasian police officers are racists, it must be noted that most of them never publicly manifest racist's tendencies, and excel in their assigned task. It is only the minority among them that are racists. But this issue is like an organ in the human body. Human beings have many organs, and if any organ is sick, it has to be diagnosed before being treated if there is to be any hope of curing it. Otherwise, if the sickness goes untreated, the person may likely pass on. In order that the minority of racists police officers be helped, not only to redeem themselves but the image of Caucasian police officers in general, they have to first of all be made to admit that they are biased in the way they treat brown or dark- skinned people. For some of them, racism has been deeply engrained in them and has become a sort of second nature. They act reflexively, without thinking. It would certainly take some time along with committed training to bring this racist behavior to a conscious level from where it can be handled.

This is why racism is a rather difficult behavior to face since, as indicated here, people rarely admit to being biased. Dr. Doreen F. Loury, the director of pan African studies at Acadia university, says there is no doubt that racism permeates every facet of our societal pores. But it becomes tragic when people allow it to destroy their profession by resorting to killing, arresting and harassing innocent people for no other reason than their God given complexion [1]. At this point it is of vital importance that we examine the nature of biases, both conscious and the unconscious ones that everyone has by virtue of being a being human. Then we must highlight the unconscious biases with a view toward making the Caucasian police officers in particular-- due to the essential nature of their job—recognize their biases to reverse the damage as well as to change their mind-set to avoid further damage. This will not only make them more professional in their assigned tasks but will equally save many lives on the roads. It is imperative to examine the notion of biases, both positive and negative, in general before focusing on the negative biases, the main purpose of undertaking this venture.

Religious Segregation

St. Paul indicates that in Christ Jesus, there is no difference between Jews and Gentiles, between slaves and free people, between men and women-- we are all one in union with Christ Jesus. "And If you belong to Christ, then you are Abraham's descendants, heirs according to the promise" (Gal.3:28-29). We are going to examine the external laws vis-a-vis the ones in person's heart.

Much has so far been said and known about the various divisions and discriminations in many parts of the world particularly here in the United States. The fifty different States within the country were somehow united without uniting the different races which make it up. Over the years, the history of immigration, socialization and ultimate discrimination has been exposed. The first immigrants to America were Europeans, many of whom were given the option of either immigrating or facing the death penalty over crimes they had committed. Earlier in this writing, the history leading to the self-assumed superiority of the pale-skinned Caucasians (erroneously called "white") over the dark or brown- skinned Africans, (the mistakenly styled "blacks") was explored. There is no doubt, through government legislation, a lot seems to have been done within the years to mitigate the disastrous effect of racism. However, it is still not fully eliminated.

Racial Segregation of the Worshipping Communities as a Continuous Perpetuation of Racism

Though the government has worked to reduced racism, not much seems to have been accomplished on the interior, the spiritual side of man in this part of the global village. In other words there has not been much conversion and convincing among worshippers to become aware that, just as thanks to the legislators, anybody can shop anywhere, worshipping God freely in any denomination by a person of any race should be commonplace. Though on some occasions an African American may visit or attend a "Caucasian Church" and vice versa, one rarely finds either being at home in "each other's church" or being free with each other following the service or Eucharistic celebration for Catholics. The fundamental question one needs to grapple with is 'If I am not at home with my fellow Christians or believers here in this world, what guarantee do I have that I am going to be at home with them in the aftermath, in heaven' ? We should bear in mind the dictum that whatever is done here on earth is equally done in the hereafter or the next place of abode. In the Our Father, the prayer that Jesus Christ taught his disciples, it is said, "thy will be done on earth as it is in Heaven".

In other words, does it dawn on any Christian that if one never learns to be at home with one's fellow human beings here on earth, it will be too late for such individual to learn to be at home with others in the hereafter? Many events in this global village of ours are didactic, so the useless murder of nine of our fellow human beings at a Bible study is an equally big lesson. Attesting to this, a group article titled "American" churches: often a reflection of the nation's racial divide", says "Last week's attack at the Emmanuel African Methodist Episcopal Church highlighted a truth about American religion and race that dates back to the 19th century; Churches are among the most segregated parts of American life". The articles quotes religious experts who affirm that the tradition of religious separation, which remained intact through the civil rights era, have proven mostly immune to progress since then. The article points out "Until Blacks and Whites pray together, US race relations are fundamentally unhealthy. There is no getting around this…Segregated Churches have often and will continue to be a direct reflection on America divided". [2]

At this point it is essential to carefully examine the book "Divided by Faith" written by Michael O. Emerson and in order to be familiar with what is currently going on regarding the adverse effects of this continued segregation of worshippers. He enumerates the practices which generate continued racial divisions in the US as increasingly covert, embedded in normal operations, avoiding direct racial terminology and invisible to most Caucasians.

According to Emerson, racism is a sheer misuse of power resulting in a diminished life opportunities for some racial groups. It changes its ideology with the constant and rational purpose of perpetuating and justifying a social system that is racialized. This includes individual overt prejudice and discrimination with racialization embedded within the normal, everyday operations of institutions. It goes without saying that religion, as structured here in America, is not only incapable of making any impact on the racialized society, but also generally maintains those historical divides as well as helping to develop new ones instead of knocking down racial barriers. In his book, Emerson says "Religion in America can serve as a moral force in freeing people but not in bringing them together as equals across racial lines [3].

However, I beg to differ with Emerson on the last cited point since, for any religion worthy of the name, necessarily links its followers to the freedom of all believers. Those who discriminate against others are never free, and so religion for the racists is not even held or seen as a moral force in freeing people. The issue of race exists because it is racialized. Who people marry, where they live, political struggles, interests and identities, etc, are all part of our racialized society and structures of racial boundaries.

Placing people in racial groups implies some form of hierarchy; we have a racialized society which, in part, allocates differential rewards by race, a fundamental cleavage defined as differences in political alignment among groups- class, gender, religion and race. Outlining three basic and connected doctrines, as free will individualism, relationalism and anti-structuralism, Emerson and Smith explain that these three things prevent white evangelism from even perceiving that there is a race problem in America in the first place. And if they do, far as they do, they typically attribute it to fabrications or people causing troubles when they shouldn't be and as such is never a focal point in their daily lived experience.

Clarification of these evangelization doctrines for a better comprehension is of vital importance here. First, freewill individualism is the idea that anything that happens is due to the free will choices of individuals and not to the larger structural constraints or influences. Accordingly racism is only a problem because of racists and prejudiced individuals. If personal prejudice is eliminated, then racism is also eliminated and so there would no longer be a problem. Second, relationalism is attributed to the sinful nature of human beings, who are made better persons via a personal relationship with Christ. At no point are larger structural problems and solutions ever contemplated. Finally, anti-structuralism is a corollary to freewill individualism and prevents one from attributing any harm, problems or malice to the nature or structure of institutions themselves. Since these systems and programs are viewed as obviating personal responsibility and not changing the hearts of individuals, they are ultimately destructive.

Definition of Bias

Bias can be defined as a preconceived or unreasoned hostility towards a particular person or a group of people or things. It is used in reference to the prejudice against a person in favor or against something or someone else. As seen above, this can be a thought about a group or individual when the individual or group is compared to another in a negative manner. Bias can also be referred to as a natural inclination to an opinion or thought that someone holds about something or against another person. Since bias is often intertwined with prejudice, it is important to examine the latter as well. Prejudice is a judgment made by an individual based on premature thoughts and is consequently removed from any study or research about the individual or group of people concerned. It is one of the negative factors challenging our global village from time immemorial. Since it promotes hatred among people, many desert one another's relationships and consequently lose their relevance.

The feelings created by prejudice include hatred, fear and insecurity and consequently creating numerous negative issues causing destruction and other various problems across the globe.

Differentiating Bias from Prejudice

It should be understood that both bias and prejudice are two disastrous factors when trying to maintain peace and harmony among human beings. While bias refers to negative thoughts of an individual or group leaning towards social settings such as politics, society, religion or economics, prejudice is the process of making a decision or judging something prematurely and relying on such a decision instead of searching for the truth about it. Bias is a preference of one thing over the other while prejudice is used when someone or something is totally rejected and hated. In brief, while bias refers to a person having any sort of influence over another in such a way that he doubts the truth about the individual or thing concerned, prejudice involves a premature judgement. Bias can be either a positive or negative opinion that one has based on that individual's experiences. It is unnatural since, it is completely devoid of objectivity concerning the person or thing in question. This causes an individual to either completely avoid or hate the person or thing or on the flip side, become addicted to and love the person or thing without any specific reason. [4]

Disregarding the Law of the Land in favor of privileges for Benefactors

While the minority in this county are abused by some Caucasian officers, some of these offices relax the laws of the land for their friends on the road or give them illegal privileges. If some of these Caucasian police officers who are technically murdering many African American young men were actually on fire doing their job by arresting those breaking the law irrespective of race, many would have appreciated what they do. But how does one reconcile the fact that some of these racist officers are playing double negative games by condoning or rather encouraging their Caucasian friends to break the law of the land while at the same time severely punishing or killing many African-Americans for actual or suspicious breaking of the law? Kathi Fedden filed a law suit on December18th,2014, against the police in Mineola, New York, for being responsible for the death of her son, Fedden Jr. whom the police officers caught drunk while driving. Instead of arresting him, the police rather drove Fedden Jr. home without any charge as a return favor for always allowing the Caucasian police officers to eat at his Deli at a very reduced price. While still drunk that night, Fedden Jr. took his mother's vehicle and got killed in a car crash [5].

Racism takes a great toll on the African American lives on one hand while on the other hand, favoritism took the life of the

Caucasian indicated here. Besides this, since it took hundred of years for a culture of dominance of the majority on the minority and all that it entails, to be built up, changing racists attitude is certainly a gradual process provided people are not being deluded into believing that all is well when in actual fact, it is just been swept under the carpet due to legislations. In other words the reasonable thing to do is to help the police officers concerned to be aware of the harm they are causing in order to find a way out, not necessarily via law suits, since in most cases they may not even be indicted by their respective grand juries. It is therefore necessary to delve into the way that will bring some amount of sanity and peace of mind to the offices concerned via job preservation and, at the same time, security of the lives of the innocent minority in this country. This is obviously going to be based on the assumption that, at least a good number of the officers involved in this criminality against the minority are doing so due to or acting out due to an unconscious or cultural/ implicit bias. Though, as some researches point out, unconscious biases develop at early stages, most of which are in-born, and through influences they are not even aware of, they may be virtually impossible to change. But as testified to by Howard Ross's personal experience, while it is admissibly difficult to eliminate all biases, it is at least possible to create an awareness of the biases within the officers concerned. Once this is done, then a dialogue on what to do about it may commence. Howard Ross points out that "dealing more effectively with unconscious bias involves something as simple as just noticing the bias"[6]. Once bias is noticed following a period of regression, something is going to trigger a past memory and the feeling associated with it. This is the way of identifying with and creating the freedom with which to choose a different pattern of behavior. This implies first of all, helping to neutralize through the creation of the awareness of its hidden existence prior to working towards its elimination. It is no doubt challenging to know the exact standard one uses for measuring changes in our unconscious biases.

Though there are some testing mechanisms that are very effective in giving feedback as to the positive or negative implicit responses to certain groups, yet they are not without challenges. Anecdotal stories of change are never definitive though they can be powerful and emotionally moving. They are often interpreted via the lens of the very mind possessing open or hidden bias: "The results that people produce, are an important metric for sure, but results can be influenced by so many variables that they are hard to attribute to any single behavioral change".[7] This warrants its continued measurement over a period of time to ensure sustainability.

Besides this, even behavioral change is never a dependable gauge for determining authentic transformational change. One has therefore to take into consideration the combination of all the things like attitude, behavior and results in order to arrive at an authentic transformation. This has to be incorporated within the training period along with an elaborate explanation of the significance of oath at the swearing-in ceremony of police officers. This is going to make them understand what they are going to be dealing with in order to define a clear set of behaviors aimed at moving the nation forward in the right direction where the life of everyone irrespective of race is respected and protected by law enforcement officers. Howard Ross points out that any movement towards working on identifying and navigating the unconscious biases during the training of the would-be officers begins with motivation. Everyone has to be made to see that there is greater purpose in being more thoughtful and less judgmental and in learning not to allow one's automatic assumptions and stereotypes run his live, since the individual is a member of the dominant group whose motivation for the change envisaged is rather limited.

The two major motivators for learning how to navigate the unconscious biases are commitment to engage in a healthy interactions among various set of people to promote equity within the community as well as justice in the society. At the core of this education is pointing out to the trainees, to the best of their understanding, how much unconscious mind influences every one, and the basic concept of how one opens up to the possibility that there may be things unknown to him/her that are going on. This does not in any way imply that the trainees have to become psychologists or neuroscientists. However accepting not to believe everything taught to be good helps toward managing biases. This is the main reason for advocating the incorporation of some sort of unconscious bias

Chapter Five

We need to take a close look at the effect of this sort of racial profile. When innocent passengers are unnecessarily abused on the way to their legitimate businesses on the basis of their race under the pretext of searching for crimes, the guilty police officers when charged and convicted should not be allowed the use of taxpayer's money to pay for such crimes (i.e. in cases when victims succeed in claiming compensation from the law suits already on the increase). Attesting to this, Michelle Conlin, reporting for Reuters says "Police misconduct claims- including law-suites against police for using the kind of excessive force that killed Garner- have risen 214 percent since 2000, while the amount the city paid out has risen 75 percent in the same period, to 464.4million in fiscal year 2012, the last year for which data is available". [1].

Racial Profiling, in other words, refers to the targeting of particular individuals by some law enforcement officers based not on their behavior but solely on their race, ethnicity, nationality or religion. It is an impermissible guideline to any degree in determining which individual to stop, detain, question or subject to other enforcement activities. It should be noted that as spelled out here, the qualifying phrase, 'impermissible use' indicates that the definition does not prohibit its use by the law enforcement agents in all circumstances. It is specifically aimed at law enforcement activities premised on an erroneous assumption that individuals of a particular race etc., are more likely to be engaged in certain types of unlawful acts than individuals from another race, ethnicity, nationality or religion. Thus it is not considered racial profiling when the law enforcement officials rely on those personal characteristics as part of a subject's description or in connection with an investigation if there is a reliable information linking a person of a particular race to a specific incident, scheme or organization. It would be understood that the race of that particular individual has nothing to do with the investigation in question. As said above, what is rather called into question is using skin color and other racial or ethnic characteristics as criteria for deciding if a person is suspicious and warranting an arrest.

As professor Harris pointed out in his 2014 June congressional testimony, "racial profiling drives a wedge between police and those they serve and this cuts off the police officers from the most important thing the police officers need to know, information about what the real problems on the ground are, who the predators are and what the community really needs which can only come from the public…when racial profiling becomes a common practice in a law enforcement agency, all of this is put in jeopardy. When one group is targeted by police, this erodes the basic elements of the relationship police need to have with the group. It replaces trust with fear and suspicion. And fear and suspicion cut off the flow of communication".[2]

Racial profiling is mostly perpetuated against African-Americans. Besides the three ongoing cases of police brutality, another case has been reported. John Crawford was seen holding a pellet gun at a Walmart in Ohio, and police automatically shot and killed him without, as the complaint file indicates, giving him time either to drop it or explain how he got it. When the grand jury refused to indict the officer for the killing, demonstration began to be staged across the country while the justice department investigated the case. From the video recently released by the family's lawyer, Michael Wright, it is rather obvious that the officer was trying to force the victim's girl friend to say something to justify the murder. He threatened to put her in jail, and accused her of drunkenness or being under the influence of drugs. It was only when she expressed her willingness to take a lie detector test or whatever the police deemed necessary that she was left off the hook. In a police report on the matter, the officer indicated that it was only later in the Walmart that he learnt the source of the gun: "I also learned while on the scene that the rifle involved was a pellet gun".

According to the limited FBI data available, racial disparities remain even in situations in which a victim gets shot wasn't attacking anyone else. From the video shown, John Crawford did not seem to be aiming at anyone before being shot by the police. 'The video which tracks Crawford as he makes his way throughout the store, first shows him walking around while talking on his phone and picking up the gun from the sporting goods aisle. It shows him pointing at the floor but at no point is the gun pointed at anything in particular, let alone pointing at anybody. Ninety seconds into the video, he moved out of the aisle as the police officers enter the store with their guns drawn and aimed. Crawford drops the gun and trips over into the rear aisle of the store. The police fired immediately upon seeing him, contrary to the claim of the prosecutor that he was shot before he dropped the gun.

The 911 call was placed by Ronald Ritchie, a Caucasian who alleged that Crawford was aiming the gun at people. As later discovered and reported, Crawford was not doing anything like that when he was shot. The arrest and subsequent death of Eric Garner over the minor offense of selling cigarettes without tax remission is another example of police brutality towards African-Americans. When the case was handed over to the Caucasian grand jury, they sided with the officers rather than indicting them. This indicates that "the officers acted properly and within the scope of the law". This testifies to the fact that racial discrimination is still as problematic as it was prior to the 1964 regulation against it. This is in line with the assertion made by the New York state Association president of criminal defense lawyers, Aaron Mysliwiec, who commented on the afore mentioned police brutality with the full backing of the grand jury saying "There are a lot of cases where the police officers don't get indicted for what looks like extreme situations". [3] The fact that the arrest was video recorded and seen by anyone who cared, proves beyond any shadow of doubt that the decision not to indict the police was racially motivated.

Besides this, a week prior to the Staten Island murder, an unarmed African American teenager, Michael Brown, was shot dead by a Caucasian police man in Ferguson, Missouri. The officer was never indicted. This obviously caused a lot of protests leading to destruction of property by some of those who joined in the protests against the non- indictment of Darren Wilson, the officer who shot Brown. Commenting on these incidents which clearly spelled out discrimination, the president, inter alia, said there is a "concern on the part of too many minority communities that law enforcement is not working with them and dealing with them in a fair way".

Setting up a commission to examine the decisions of the two aforementioned incidents in search of for a way forward, Obama continues "We are not going to let off until we see a strengthening of accountability that exists between our communities and our law enforcement" [4].

The accountability in question has already started surfacing when a Baltimore Police officer, Vincent Cosom, was caught in surveillance beating an African American, Kollin Truss, in June 2014. On Friday, May 15th, 2015, Cosm was sentenced to six months imprisonment after pleading guilty to the assault. And on June 5th, 2015, a jury consisting of eleven women and one man convicted Mary O'Callaghan, a Caucasian police officer, of felony assault after she repeatedly kicked a handcuffed African American woman, Alicia Thomas. Thomas later died at the hospital in Los Angeles. Though charged with assault, and not directly on Thomas's death, O' Callaghan has been relieved of her duty without pay pending administrative hearing. However, her kicking cannot be excluded as a contributing factor in Thomas's death, for what she will be soon charged. Commenting on the charge, Los Angeles chief of police, Charlie Beck, says "It is always disappointing when an officer fails to uphold the high standards and professionalism shown by thousands of LAPD daily". He indicated his appreciation of their partnership with the District Attorney's office "to ensure that officers who operate outside the law, and tarnish our badge, are held accountable". The District Attorney, Jackie Lacey said that she was pleased that the jury agreed with their assessment of the evidence [5].

The recent release of the video portraying the deadly shooting of seventeen- year old Cedrick Chatman, an African American for sixteen times within fifteen seconds alleged to have attempted stealing a vehicle by a Caucasian police officer, Kevin Fry on January 7th,2013, is another confirmation of young African-Americans being wantonly murdered by Caucasian police officers. On January 7th.2013, Chatman was shot sixteen times within fifteen seconds for allegedly attempting to steal a vehicle. According to a Caucasian Police officer, Kevin Fry, per the January15th, 2016 report, Kevin has been charged with first degree murder and held on a $1.5million bond. Fry had pleaded not guilty to the charge on the grounds, that he feared for his life when he assumed that the lap top that Cedrick was carrying was a gun.

It goes without saying that some of the Caucasians attorneys in this country are co-conspirators to the murdering of the African-Americans by their fellow Caucasians in police uniforms. This is buttressed by the fact that the city attorneys had struggled to keep the video surveillance footage unleased, claiming that its release could taint the jury pool if the pending case went on trial. As would be expected, the release of the video has spurred numerous protests by the Black Lives matter activists who are fighting for a reform and an end to institutionalized racism in America particularly in Chicago. In a similar vein, in October 2014 Laquan McDonald--, a seventeen year-old African American living in Chicago—was fatally shot sixteen times by a Caucasian police officer named Van Dyke. Following the release of the video Dash cam to the public, the major of the city, Rahm Emmanuel, fired the police chief, Garry McCarthy, saying that it is an "undeniable fact that the public trust on the leadership has been shaken and eroded". Jason Van Dyke, the murderer, was charged with first degree murder. He had already been released from prison after paying $150,000 of the $1.5million dollar bond he had previously been held on prior to the release of the video. As Major Rahm Emmanuel points outs: "any case of excessive force or abuse of authority undermines the entire force and the trust we must build with every community in the city"[6].

Emmanuel then created a task force mandating the acting police chief, John Escalante, to safeguard public safety and restore trust between the community and the police. The reform initiated here included policy changes aimed at a better training of police officers on how to respond to and resolve tense situations without resorting to deadly force. As Emmanuel says, "the reforms are meant to inject some humanity into the work of our police department and our police officers"[7].

Cincinnati and Seattle are good models for the reforms in question. For example, in response to complaint that Cincinnati police stop and frisk minority drivers more often than the majority Caucasians, the department implemented the use of "contact cards" which required officers to fill out with details such as the race of every person in vehicles which they stopped and checked on the road. The departments also discarded the previous policy that new recruits had to be thirty-five years old, instead stipulating that all recruits must have college degrees. Allied with this, in 2002, the Citizens Complaint Authority was created to conduct independent reviews for each incident in which a Cincinnati police officer used deadly force. The idea was to create easy identification of officers with a history of violence and racism in the state [8]. On December 8th, 2014, via the office of the federal attorney General, the federal government issued guidelines banning law enforcement from profiling on the basis of race, religion and other characteristics. The Justice Department hopes these guidelines could be a model for local departments as the federal government tackles questions about the role it plays in policing. This is an expansion of the plan which the Bush administration formulated but never implemented a decade ago. However, while the Civil

Rights movement welcomes it, they are disappointed that the guidelines exempt security screening at airports and border check points, and they are not binding on local and state agencies. The then attorney general, Eric Holder was scheduled at one time to present the idea to local and state police departments with the hopes of getting them to be a part of it. Essentially, what is covered by the guidelines include: the FBI, the drug enforcement administration, the bureau of alcohol and tobacco and state officers serving on joint task forces alongside federal agents.

White Trial Judges' Biases against African-Americans

It has been made known that some of the Caucasian trial judges are never fair in their sentencing African-Americans brought before them. Affirming this. Michelle Alexander, a civil rights attorney, says that America's criminal justice system perpetuates racial inequities. Statistically, based on the Sentencing Project, African-Americans make up 12% of the nation's drug users, but represent 34% of those arrested for drug offences and 45% of those in state prison for such offence as of 2005.

In her book, "The New Jim Crow: Mass Incarceration in the age of Colorblindness," Alexander chronicled how African American youths are less likely to be drug users. According to her, Caucasian students use cocaine and heroin at seven times the rate of their African American counterparts and use crack at eight times the rate, based on a study from the National Institute on Drug Abuse. [9]

Besides this, according to Eugene Jarecki, "We live for a very long time with the idea that crack is a black drug and powder is a white drug, and the actual facts that I discovered when I made the film is that crack was never a black drug. The majority of crack users in the United States of America are and always have been white. Once you know the fact, it reminds you how much propaganda has hoodwinked us 40 years about these drugs." But as of 2002, more than 80% Americans sentenced under federal crack cocaine laws, were African-Americans, according to the Sentencing Project. This Project has found also that African-American drug offenders have a 20% greater chance of being sentenced to prison than Caucasian drug offenders.[10]

Supremacist Murdering

The unimaginable shooting resulting in the deaths of nine African-Americans on June 17th, 2015, is a rather clear example of supremacist murder. These victims were shot while participating in a Bible study in the historically African American Church, Methodist Episcopal Church, in Charleston, South Carolina. Their murderer, a 21- year old Dylann Storm Roof committed this unspeakable act on the grounds that "blacks were taking over the world". Commenting on this Ahmad Syafi, a prominent Indonesian said: "People all over the world believed that racism had gone from the US when Barack Obama was elected to lead the superpower twice. But the Charleston shooting has reminded us that in fact, the seeds of racism still remain and were embedded in the hearts of small communities there, and can explode at any time, like a terrorist act by an individual"[11].

Twenty-one- year- old Yuka Christine Koshino, a student of political science at the university of Tokyo, remarked on how devastated she was at the shootings particularly having participated in racism awareness campaigns while studying in the university of California, Berkeley. These interactions had given her hope of improving the situation. The Charleston shooting and many other similar shootings in this country are a pointer to the fact that some existing racial structures and attitudes are not stagnating but rather nurturing racism. [12]

During an interview with Marc Maron, June 19th published on the internet on June 22nd,2015, President Obama said that "while the country has made a great effort in reducing discrimination, the legacy of slavery and Jim Crow, discrimination still exits in institutions and casts a long shadow, and it's still part of our DNA that's passes on. We are not cured of it, and it is not just a matter of not being polite and not saying the N- word. That's not the measure of whether racism still exits. It's not just a matter of obvert discrimination" [13].

The president indicated how frustrated he has become over the unwillingness of the Congress to keep guns out of the hands of those venting their frustration on innocent African- Americans.

He said: "I tell you right after Sandy Hook, Newton, when 20-6 year- olds were gunned down and Congress literally does nothing, yeah, that's the closest I came to feeling disgusted".[14] The then GOP presidential candidate, and long experienced neurosurgeon, Ben Carson said that it was important to diagnose the racial problems responsible for the murder of the nine people in the Charleston immediately, rather than engage in an "interpretive dance" so as not to offend some Americans. "Let's call this sickness what it is, so we can get on with the healing. If this were a medical disease and all the doctors recognized the symptoms but refused to make the diagnosis for fear of offending the patient, we could call it madness"[15]. Obviously referring to his then- fellow presidential candidates, who were dancing around the issue in order not to offend the supremacists when voting, he continued, "But there are people who are claiming that they can lead this country, who dare not call this tragedy an act of racism, a hate crime, for fear of offending a particular segment of the electorate"[16].

Hilary Clinton, a Democratic presidential candidate rhetorically asks "How is it possible that we as a nation we still allow guns to fall into the hands of people whose hearts are filled with hate?" This brings home the fact that racism, besides being entrenched in the minds of the supremacists, is also used in playing politics, and this can't augur well with America.

Institutional Racism

Institutional racism is a pattern in all walks of life including housing, business, employment, professional associations, religion. Media etc. The effect is that it perpetuates and maintains an unfair power, influence and better sense of well-being of one race over others. Since it mostly originates from established forces in society, it receives far less public criticism than individual racism, which is destructive to humanity through more subtle ways. There are different ways in which racism in various ways is manifested. For example, a professor at the university of Chicago, recently wanted to show in a practical way how racism is still a part of our society particularly in terms of employment opportunities. He sent five thousand fictitious resumes in response to one thousand three hundred wanted advertisements. Each resume listed identical qualifications, with one variation- some applicants had Anglo-sounding names like "Brendan" while others had black-sounding names like "Jamal". It was confirmed that applicants with Anglo-sounding names were 50% more likely to be invited for interviews than their black sounding counterparts. The only point that remains in contention is whether the interviewers who did not choose applicants with black- sounding names were motivated by racial bias, as UCLA researcher, L. Ames questions. However he is right in affirming that racial biases can in many ways be more destructive than outright racism, since they are harder to spot and consequently harder to combat.

Crystal Morten, a history professor at Dickinson college in Carlisle, Pennsylvania affirms that the impact of racism is killing people of color. "We don't have time to tend to the emotional wounds of others, not when violence against people of color is the national status quo"[17].

Police ---Police profiled in Civil Attire

It is known that Caucasian police brutality and racial profiling of African-Americans are not restricted only to civilians because most African American Police officers experience the same brutality when they are off duty and in civilian attire. In other words it is like the words of Jesus Christ ring true: any kingdom divided against itself can never stand.(Mark 3:24). Harold Thomas, a decorated detective who had recently retired narrated how around 1am on August 20th, 2012, he was leaving a birth day party at a night club. He was stopped by two Caucasian police officers who got into an altercation with him. They beat him up, smash his head against the hook of their vehicle, spurn him to the ground and put him in hand-cuffs. Remarking on the incident, Thomas said "If I was white, it wouldn't have happened". He indicated that he had filled a lawsuit against the city over the incident [18].

This is one of the many known cases of racial profiling of African-Americans police officers by their Caucasian counterparts, confirming what most of Thomas's fellow African American officers recently mentioned in interviews. Some African- American officers that have been racially profiled and attacked by their Caucasian colleagues reported the incident to their superiors only to be met with adverse consequences. Others, however fearing such adverse consequences, kept the incidents to themselves. "Reuters interviewed 25 African American male officers on the NYPD, 15 of whom are retired and 10 of them were still serving. All but one said that when off duty and out of uniform, they had been victims of racial profiling, which refers to using race or ethnicity as grounds for suspecting someone of having committed a crime." According to the officers interviewed, this racial profiling included "being pulled over for no reason, having their heads slammed against their cars, getting guns brandished in their faces, being thrown into prison vans and experiencing stop and frisks while shopping[19]. Vanessa Westley, a twenty- five year- veteran of the Chicago police Department revealed her fear regarding her Caucasian counterpart's recent shooting of young black men. As a single black mother of an eighteen year-old son, herself, she rhetorically asks "Do I have to walk the same course as any other mother who has a black son"? "Yes I do". She adds that it is a little harder because she goes to work in the same system that she is concerned about. Acknowledging the reality, she says that the badge does not make others immune to the types of incidents that have made headlines in recent months, most notably the fatal killing of Laquan. She and her colleague recalled a time when they were pulled over without reason when they were off duty; what apparently saved them was being recognized as colleagues by the officer on patrol [20]. The majority of the officers interviewed, said that they had been pulled over multiple times while driving. Five had guns pulled on them. According to one of the African-American police officers, Adam, who would not give his last name in order not to be identified since he is still in the service, talking about race is regarded as a taboo within the police force and therefore falling to instruct their officers on how to police in a racially charged environment. Lt. LeRonne Armstrong, a thirty-nine year- old African American officer points out the need for police officers to change, for it is necessary that his colleagues treat their children with dignity and respect. Black officers, as already indicated, equally experience racism or racial issues which they are forced to tolerate, such as stereotypes on the job as well as confrontation by their Caucasian colleagues. Besides this, Black plain-clothed or undercover police officers have been shot by their Caucasian colleagues as in the case of Omar J. Edwards, an NYPD officer killed in 2009, while chasing a man who had broken into his car. Kevin A. Minor, a St. Louis county police recruitment and field training officer recounted how he was followed around a discount store by a Caucasian officer while trying to shop. It is against this background that President Barack Obama affirmed during his interview with Black Entertainment Television that a variety of factors from training to subconscious racial fears have combined to create a national problem that is going to require a national solution [21].

Mind set and Criminality

In the aforementioned racial profiling, some of the Caucasian police officers involved in the undue checking, arresting or killing of African-Americans have the mindset that they are criminals. In their biased minds, every African American person especially young men, is a criminal although about ninety percent of the people searched on the road have committed no crime.

If America is to be what it has set out to be, a place where everyone is free to aspire to and achieve his legitimate goals, much has to be done to bring some sanity into the law enforcement department as a whole, otherwise the plague in question is going to destroy the nation.

Everyone to be on board as a solution towards this conflict.

The police chief, David Brown, in Dallas points out that the reason as to why there is so much of the tensions between the Police Departments and minority communities that they serve is because the police is asked to do too much while the populace does too little themselves.[22] Analyzing this assertion, president Obama points out how the country underinvest in decent schools, allows poverty to fester so that the entire neighborhood offers no prospect for gainful employment. It refuses to fund drug- treatment and mental health programs, flood communities with so many guns that it is easier for a teenager to buy a glock than get his hand on a computer or even open a book. And then the police are told: "you're the social worker, you're the parent, you're the teacher, you're the drug counselor", telling them to keep the neighborhood in check at all cost and do so without causing political blowback or inconvenience. When periodically the tensions boil over, people feign surprise.

What the nation needs now, more than anything else is consensus that can only be arrived at through commitment and mutual respect. This, first of all, entails on the part of the police officers love for their profession, love accompanied by compassion. This is what can make anyone especially a police officer that manifests racist's behavior to open his heat and to see his own son reflected "in that teenager with a hoodie who is kind of goofing off but not dangerous, and the teenager may see in the police officer the same words and values and authority of his parents".[23] This is the practical step to be taken in order to bring about reconciliation of every race within the country. With this sort of openness, the police officers, in a practical way, acknowledge that like others, they are not perfect and as such by asking that racial bias should never be manifested especially when on duty, is never an attack on the cops but an effort to live up to their highest ideals demanded by their profession.[24]

Life as the most precious and unique gift

Every normal human being does not need to be told of the value and the importance of human life. This is the rationale behind doing everything humanly possible to protect it. The uniqueness of human life in particular is so central that no human being despite commendable work done by scientists, none has ever, on his own, been able to bring about the existence of another human being out of nothing. Among the gifts bestowed on man, is the one of using one's intellect to know his creator, as well as the freedom to acknowledge his creator by obeying his regulations which ensure his fulfilment as a human being. It is against this background that man turns to the source of every life, and the creator of every other thing both within and beyond our universe, God. Since God is the space setter, He alone who creates, has an authority to bring one's life to an end as long as this universe is concerned. This explains the reasoning behind recent leaders of the Catholic Church, beginning especially with Pope John Paul II, have been very vocal against capital punishment. With new technical development, a criminal of any sort can be successfully confined to prison for life. Consequently it is no longer necessary to put hardened criminals to death. Many countries in general and many states in this country in particular, no longer allow capital punishment. Unfortunately some individuals are playing the God, making of themselves 'gods and goddesses' when they kill fellow human beings ranging from the innocent ones in the womb down to racist police officers on the streets. By doing so they turn against the creator who strictly forbids us from taking away what is never in our power to dispose of, as well as the human community that loses the services of those murdered. By resorting to this various ways of killing fellow human beings, the murderers are equally going against the basic human principle that no one takes what does not belong to him. In other words murderers are equally thieves except that when they steal they never own but rather destroy the lives unduly stolen.

The danger of losing God's guiding hand in the land.

America has been one of the countries that freely acknowledge God as their creator deserving of being followed and obeyed. This is why the founding fathers of this nation placed America under His care and guardianship when, in her currency, Dollar notes, it is written "In God we trust". There is no doubt that the God in whom this country trusts, has all along been protecting and blessing this land with an abundance of resources. But some of our contemporaries are not only taking God for granted but they are also turning agnostics or outright atheists manifested both in words and deeds. Before glancing at the agnostic or atheistic altitudes rapidly gaining ground here in this country, it is worthwhile briefly looking at the practice of many regular worshippers or rather the church attendees as against the faithful i.e. those who not only learn about the demands of God from His creatures but freely embrace the faith that requires that God be worshipped in spirit and in truth. It is therefore nothing new or unfamiliar to Christians that the explanation of Jesus Christ on how to worship God is that of loving God with one's life (incorporating one's whole heart, being, strength, mind) and one's neighbor as he loves himself. However, when the Jewish attorney to whom Jesus was addressing asked for an explanation as to whom one's neighbor, within the context, would be, Jesus pointed out (through a parable of neighbor-ness or good Samaritan) that a fellow human being, irrespective of color, race, nationality, language, gender or occupation, is one's neighbor. And as such everyone should be treated with love and respected as one loves himself, his wife, children or friend. (Lk.10:25-37). Besides this the golden rule for every person states: "Do unto others as you would have them do unto you". Adding that the whole law and teaching of God is summarized here, Jesus says: "There is the laws and the prophets". (Mtt.7,12) If therefore as, it is very clear in this biblical texts, everyone in the entire universe is a neighbor to each other and needs to be loved and respected, how would someone reconcile the senseless killing of some African-Americans on the streets. Would the Caucasian police officers involved in such a crime love to see their relatives killed under the same circumstance?

An important question is if human life is that important that even some countries and states in this country never tamper with, is there any set of human beings whose lives never matter? This is rather a rhetorical question since every human life matters including lives of criminals as explained above. But when some public servants like the racist Caucasians who happen to be police officers without being convinced that their main assignment is to protect lives and property and not to destroy them, then it stands to reason to remind the racists that every life including "Black life" matters. Consequently every person from any race or nationality should be treated with respect and accorded the dignity he deserves even if he violates some traffic regulations.

It is in this light that the highest law enforcement officer in the country, President Obama uses as an example, the life of Alton Sterling murdered by a police officer, that the pain of Sterling's family, along with those of his friends and co-workers who described him as a very caring man should be heard by his murderer. The President reminds everyone that though no one has control of everything, "yet we have control of how we treat each other". [25]

Michael Jordan, an African American NBA champion and basketball legend, says that he can no longer remain silent about the worsening of racial tension. And so Jordan decides not only to make his voice heard but also takes a practical step towards putting an end to the senseless killings on both sides of the divide. Running his memory lane of "the recent police killings of Alton Sterling in Baton Rouge, Louisiana State, and that of Philando Castile in Falcon Heights, Minnesoda, the police shooting of North Miami behavioral therapist, Charles Kinsey as he lays on his back with his hands thrust in trying to coax an autistic patient back into a mental health center; the killing of five police officers by a lone gun man at an otherwise peaceful Black Lives Matter, etc., Michael says: "I was raised by my parents who taught me to love and respect people regardless of their race or background. So

I am saddened and frustrated by the divisive rhetoric and racial tensions that seem to be getting worse as of late. I know this country is better than that, and I can no longer stay silent. We need to find solutions that ensure that people of color receive fair and equal treatment and that police officers- who put their lives on the line every day to protect us all- are respected and supported....I have decided to speak out in the hope that we can come together as Americans, and through peaceful dialogue and education, achieve constructive change".[26]. He donates some substantial amount of money to two organizations, the International Association of Chiefs of Police's newly established institute for Community Police Relations and the NAACP Legal Defense Fund, the nation's oldest civil rights law organization, in support of its ongoing work of reforms aimed at building trust and respect between communities and law enforcement. The donation is intended to help both organizations make a positive impact on the society.

If America is authentically "God's own country" as she is often described, why wouldn't someone feel His presence in this land, via at least, certain comportments on the part of the citizenry as a confirmation of such an assertion? The atheistic attitude is not only manifested by this comparative fraction of Caucasian police officers on the streets, it is rather gradually pervading the life style of many Americans especially some of those entrusted with the responsibility regulating the affairs of this country. Beginning with the Supreme Court of the land which formally endorsed the murdering of innocent children in the womb, abortion, in 1973 till 2015 when the same Court endorsed same sex marriage. This, in other words, is a way of saying that since abortion was not effective enough to put an end to God's mandate "be fruitful and multiply and fill the earth" (Gen. 1,28), through responsible child-bearing, the Court, therefore gave a license or official recognition to same sex union abnormally termed 'marriage'. In a way, this is an attempt at nullifying the creator's law on marriage, the union of man with a woman capable of procreation. No matter under what logic someone operates, one has to find out whether some members in the Supreme Court, by virtue of the adjective "Supreme" attached to the highest court of the country, in which they earn a living, are replacing the unique Supreme Law Giver-God- by their counter laws in 'God's own nation', America.

Since America is comprised of three components of powers, the Executive, the Legislative and the judiciary, some Americans seeing the atheistic hand writing on the wall, are voicing out their concerns regarding the sort of candidates aspiring to lead the country.. On July 19th, speaking at the GOP Convention, official nomination of the GOP presidential candidate, Ben Carson, observed a coupe d'etat being staged against God in His 'own country'. And as such since, He is too powerful to battle with the coupe d'etat plotters, (i.e. atheistic or agnostic politicians) God was gradually abandoning America to her whips and caprices. Carson says: "This nation where our founding document, the Declaration of Independence, talks about certain inalienable rights that come from our creator… This is a nation where our pledge of allegiance says we are one nation under God. This is a nation where every coin in our pocket and every bill in our wallet says 'in God We Trust'. He cautions against electing someone most likely to lead the nation further away from God. [27]

Inclusiveness of every race, nationality, complexion in this global village.

No individual chooses to be born into any culture, race, country or tribe with a particular complexion. Even one's parents can never make such a choice. All that parents choose, in most cases, is that of begetting a child or children. Nowadays, however couples, thanks to scientific development, may choose the gender of the child they want but cannot choose to have a particular child. The choice of a particular individual is made only by the creator, God, who in his wisdom, chooses to call forth an individual into being: "You did not choose me, no, but I chose you to go out and bear fruits, fruits that will last…" (Jn.15,16) Therefore every human being coming into this world is at the receiving end from the creator primarily and secondarily from one's parents through whose biological components the individual is formed at conception. Besides this, as already dealt at length in the first chapter of this book, God is quite aware that variety makes life meaningful, this is the rationale behind creating the same set of human beings in various complexions, races, nationalities, tribes, languages; natural endowments like height, weight or talents such as one's IQ enabling someone to study and embark upon any profession that the particular individual chooses, the only choice an individual can make and subsequently applies himself to. If that is the case, why then would people be so concerned about the particular complexion of others let alone abusing their profession by killing those who never look like them?

Conclusion

Education extends from the cradle to the grave and as such a lot of what people originally thought they knew turns out via further insight to be incorrect and as such when more investigations are done the truth emerges to dispel one's past ignorance. If this is the case in scientific issues one would imagine what happens when it comes to mere human perceptions. And so in case of racial discrimination particularly in America, this write-up unfolds the false claim that the complexion of any human being is white and that the authentic color of Caucasians is pale while those from African background is brown. Even if there were to be people with white complexion, white color as found in material things like clothing, vehicles, etc., it has never ever been thought to be superior to other colors. No one has ever been for example charged extra amount exclusively on the basis of color of any item bought but rather on its quality. As Martin Luther King, Jr. rightly points out, it is not the color of the skin but the content of one's character that matters and as such ought to be valued. On the other hand, experience affirms the dictum that empty vessel makes the loudest noise implying that those who alleged that they are superior based on the color of their skin are those offering nothing to the society other than parambulating themselves on the street falsely claiming that they are whites. This false notion has done untold damage to this country not only through uncalled-for shedding of innocent blood on the streets, but also the deprivation of families of their loved ones by some of the Caucasian police officers paid by the state to protect lives and properties. Investigations reveal that racism is now as bad as it was before the commencement of the civil right movement exempt that it is much more veiled than what was the case in the past. And as such everyone particularly public figures or aspirants to public offices in the land affirm of its being very much around the nook and cranny of the country. Expressing his frustrations towards his Republican Political Party on which he was the only African American among the contenders to the presidency, Ben Carson, during an interview with Trush published on Yahoo internet on February 24,2016, said when asked the last time he personally experienced racism: "you don't have to go too far. I think the way I am treated by the left is racism. Yeah because they are saying because you are black, you have to think a certain way, and if you don't think that way, you are uncle Tom. You are worthy of every horrible epithet they can come up with, whereas, if I weren't black, then I would just be a Republican". [1]. Though racism has permeated every fiber of Caucasian American neighborhood, this book still opines that a good training of police officers can pave a way towards making the Caucasians in general and their police officers as a whole, less opinionated regarding their racist's tendency. Testifying to the racist attitude of Caucasian judges, Jeff Guo, in an article published on February 24,2016, points out that in, a laboratory tests, researches have shown that "white trial judges, like most white Americans, hold implicit biases against black people and can only overcome those prejudices with conscious effort". [2]

Foot Notes

Chapter One

1. Jerald F.Dirks, Muslims in American History: A forgotten legacy, ISBN-1-59008-0440, p.204

2. Patrick N. Minges, Slavery in the Keetoowah society & the defining of a people,1855-1887,psychology press, p.27. (ISBN 978-0-415-9486-8

3. Ibid.

4. Cf. Dorothy A. Mays, Women in early America, 2008 ABC CLIO; ISBN978-1-85709-429-5.

5. Plessy V. Ferguson, 163 US357(1896) in Mekenna, George, edi., A Guide to the Constitution that delicate balance, New York, 1984

6. Cf. Civil Rights Acts signed by president Lyndon B. Johnson on July,1964.

7. Ibid

8. Liza Vos, Affirmative Action in htc://www yahoo.com

Chapter Two

1. Princeton's word net.

2. Martin Luther King, Jr. Quotes.

3. Ibid

4. Oxford Advanced Learner's Dictionary, Sixth Edition, P. 878.

5. Luke Visconti, reply to" Is people of color offensive"/diversity INC.com, May 22nd.2007.

6. Cf. President Barak Obama's excerpts of the interview released on December17[th],2014, in htt.//www.yahoo.com

7. Ibid

8. Cf. excerpts from the first Lady, Mrs. Michelle Obama, Commencement address, Tuskegee University. Alabama, May 9th,2015.

9. Ibid

10. Jim Grimsley, "White Americans are nearly as blind to racism as ever in - htt://www.latimes.com/opinion/op-ed/la-oe-02239.

11. Cf. Devin Dwyer, Obama on race, Wednesday 17th, May 2014.

12. Ibid.

13. Ibid

Chapter Three

1. Jess. Row, Op. cit. 1.Jennifer Eberhard & Jason Okonofua,(Stanford psychologists) Racial Stereotypes as factors behind more African American students being punished more than their Caucasian counterparts I schools.

2. Melinda Anderson, "White means right, Black means lack" in the Psychology of Black & white, 2014. P. 79.

3. Michael Walsh, 'Civil right activist' Rachel Dolezal, pretending to be black in http://www.cbs, June12,2015.

4. Ibid.

5. Ibid.

6. Ibid.

7. Abdul-Jabbar, in online column, Time Magazine

8. Blair L.M. Kelley, "Race is a social construct"

9. Freund Thomas, "Rachel Doleza, the debate over identity & Charleston, Chicago Tribune in http://wwwyahoo.com, June 19th,2015

10. Ibid.

11. Tara Satmayer, "Why the fascination with Rachel Dolezal in http://www.cnn yahoo.com, June 24th,2015

12. Ibid.

13. Jeff Yang, op. cit.

14. Jess Row, Op. cit.

15. Sophia Nelson, op. cit.

16. Michaela Angela Davis, op. cit.

17. Dean Obeidallah, op. cit.

18. David Brown, cited by President Barack Obama in his speech at Dallas Police Memorial, in ABC News by Noah Fitzgerel July 12, 2016.

19. President Barack Obama, Speech at Dallas Police Memorial, op.cit.

20. David Brown, cited by President Barack Obama in his Speech at Dallas Police Memorial, in ABC News Reported by Noah Fitzgerel, July 12th,2016.

21. Charring Ball, "SORRY MICHELLE.BUT THE 'STING' OF RACISM DID CHANGE YOU" in ABC News May 12th,2015

22. Ibid

23. Howard Ross. Op. cit.

24. Howard Ross, op. cit.

25. Ibid.

26. Kelly Walch, Black Criminal Stereotypes & Racial profiling in the Journal of contemporary Criminal Justice 23, no. 3, August 2007 (276-88).

27. Ibid

28. Devah Pager, Bruce Western & Bark Bonikwoski, Discrimination in low wage Labor Market: A Field Experiment, in American Sociological Review, 74 Oct.2009. 777-99

29. Howard Ross, op. cit.

30. Roll May, "The Courage to Create", New York, Norton, 1975

31. Howard Ross, op. cit p.117.

32. Gordon Allport, The Nature of Prejudice, New York, Perseus Books Publishing, 1979, p.74.

33. A personal testimony of a teenage African-American given on a video recording about the brutality of a Caucasian Police officer, Eric Casebolt, when African-American children were playing following the end of the year party in Houston Texas, June 8th,2015.

Chapter Four

1. Doreen E. Loury, Racism without racists in http://www.cnn.com, Nov.27th,2014

2. Michael O.Emerson, cited by Richard Valdmanis in American Churches: Often a reflection of the nation's racial divide, in http://www.cnn.com, June 21st,2015.

3. Ibid

4. Cf. Andrew in an article posted on http://www.cnn.com,May 6th,2011.

5. Mom sues cops for not arresting her drunk son in Associated Press Interview, Dec.2014.

6. Howard Ross, op. cit., P. 72

7. Ibid

Chapter Five

1. Cf. Michelle Conlin, "Off duty, black cops in New York feel threat from fellow police, December, Dec.23rd.2014.

2. Prof. Davis Harris, Testimony before the House judiciary Committee, sub, committee on Constitution, Civil Rights and Civil Liberties. Ending Racial Profiling necessary for public safety and protection of CIVIL Rights, June17th, 2010.

3. A brief Speech made by the president, Barak Obama, on television broadcasted by CNN channel, Dec.3rd,2014.

4. President Barak Obama, Interviewed By Marc Maron on Febrary 19th & Published June 22nd,2015.

5. Charlie Beck & Jackie Lacey in Tami Adollah on Assault in deathly arrest, Htt:// www yahoo.com, June 6th,2015.

6. Rahm Emmanuel fires police chief, Garry McCarthy, Dec.2015 in http://www. nytines.com/2015/12/02/us/Chicago-police.

7. Ibid.

8. Caithin Dickson, "Chicago looks to other cities for guidance on police reform, in yahoo news, Dec.30th,2015

9. Michelle Alexander in 'Criminal injustice': The percentage of African-Americans in prison, reported by Morgan Morgan Whitaker, MSNBC, Sept.23rd,2013

10. Eugene Jarecki, 'Criminal injustice': The percentage of African-Americans in Prison, reported by Morgan Whitaker, MSNBC, Sept. 23rd,2013.

11. Cf. Ahmad Suafi, South Carolina shootings in US Today, June 24th,2015.

12. Cf. Christine Koshino, South Carolina shooting in US Today, June,2015

13. Barak Obama, interviewed by Marc Maron on February 19th but published on Yahoo internet on June 22nd, 2015.

14. Ibid.

15. Ben Carson, on racism, http://wwwusatoday.com /story/opinion/2015-06/22 ben carson –south Carolina shooting –column/29074387, June24[th],2015.

16. Ibid.

17. Hilary Clinton, on racism,South Carolina Shooting, June 24th,2015.

18. Crystal Morton in httpp://www.yahoo news.com

19. Ibid

20. Harold Thomas, (edi.) Ross Colvin, "Off duty black cops in New York threat from fellow police. In yahoo.com, Dec.23rd,2014.

21. Vanessa Westley, "Black Chicago cops fear for their children tooin racially profiled by colleagues in http://atlantablack star.com, Jan.13th,2016.

22. Kevin A. Minor, "Off duty black cops in New York threat from fellow police, Dec.23rd.2014.

23. David Brown, cited by President Barack Obama in his Speech at the Dallas Police Memorial, July 12th,2016

24. President Barack Obama, Full Speech Address at the Dallas Police Memorial, reported by Noah Fitzerel in ABC News, July 12th.2016.

25. Ibid.

26. Michael Jordan, "I can no longer stay silent", in Undefeated Magazine, by DanDevine, July 25th, 2016.

27. Ben Carson, GOP Convention Address, July 19th. 2016

Conclusion

1. Ben Carson, Interview with Trash Magazine, February 24th,2016

2. Jeff Guo, "White Trial Judges & Implicit Racism against Blacks".Washington Post, February 24th,2016.

www.ingramcontent.com/pod-product-compliance
Lightning Source LLC
Chambersburg PA
CBHW020535290526

45786CB00002B/896